Sociological and Psychological Aspects of Information Literacy in Higher Education

Teresa Y. Neely

The Scarecrow Press, Inc.
Lanham, Maryland, and London
2002

SCARECROW PRESS, INC.

Published in the United States of America
by Scarecrow Press, Inc.
4720 Boston Way, Lanham, Maryland 20706
www.scarecrowpress.com

4 Pleydell Gardens, Folkestone
Kent CT20 2DN, England

British Library Cataloguing in Publication Information Available

Library of Congress Cataloging-in-Publication Data Available

ISBN 0-8108-4105-3 (cloth: alk. paper)

♾™ The paper used in this publication meets the minimum requirements of
American National Standard for Information Sciences—Permanence of
Paper for Printed Library Materials, ANSI/NISO Z39.48-1992.
Manufactured in the United States of America.

For Vaughn and Yvonne
because they inspire me
to laugh
to cry
to love
to be

Contents

Figures

Tables

Foreword

The concatenation of knowledge and skills necessary to deal success-fully with the modern information environment is what many ob-servers have come to call "information literacy." The basic idea is that for a person to be involved in the pursuit of formal knowledge, he or she must necessarily be skilled in locating, evaluating, and otherwise managing information. The basic problem is that while this notion is among the most popular ideas in professional library circles today, it is one about which we know remarkably little.

From the perspective of library and information science, there are at least a couple of reasons for this state of affairs. The first reason why we do not know nearly enough, if we know much at all, about informa-tion literacy is that the notion itself is a construct that encompasses an array of issues daunting enough to have warned off more than a few good researchers. The second reason is cultural. The hard truth is that librarians have a curious disdain for the research of their peers. They cleave instead to a quixotic blend of anecdote and prescription, and they have a longstanding tendency to squelch debate by raising certain issues to a status resembling that of an article of faith. The information literacy "debate" is a prime example of both these tendencies and their untoward effects.

There are prescriptions aplenty, in the form of articles, books, conference papers, and policy statements. But few questions have been asked, and even fewer questions unclouded by the moral certainties of professional library practice. As a result, we don't know exactly what information literacy is or how it is attained. We don't know how it may be related to other aspects of learning (and teaching). We don't know the extent to which context is an influence. Nor do we understand how new media or new forms of access effect it. Indeed, a reasonable person could not help but wonder if librarians and library educators have been asking the right questions at all.

This is the state of affairs that Teresa Neely decided to address. Her work rests on a disarmingly simple idea that what we call information literacy is defined ultimately and essentially by the ability to perform relevance judgments. Now, because the subject of relevance judgments has proven themselves to be one of considerable opaqueness, Neely elected to deal not with the judgments themselves, focusing instead on the sociological and psychological factors that we presume to be formative.

Neely's findings speak for themselves. Less obvious is the distinct possibility that what she has done is to deflect the course of professional dialogue regarding information literacy toward a more inductive, more empirical phase, and one that will lead us to a meaningful understanding of what it means to be information literate.

Christinger Tomer
University of Pittsburgh
June 27, 2001

Chapter 1

Investigating Information Literacy: An Empirical Approach

Defining Information Literacy

Information literacy is an abstract construct first mentioned in the library and information science literature by Zurkowski in 1974, who used the term in a document to the National Commission on Libraries and Information Science (NCLIS). Zurkowski announced the establishment of a national program to achieve universal information literacy by 1984. Until the late 1980s, there was very little consensus in the literature on a definition for this concept, or what it meant for the educational process at all levels. In 1989, the American Library Association's (ALA) current president appointed a committee to produce a report on the concept which resulted in a fairly vague but standard definition. In 1992(a), Doyle's dissertation reported on an expanded definition; however, this was the sole investigation of information literacy empirical based research that had been conducted at that point.

Information literacy as a concept encompasses the ability to access, evaluate, and use information effectively and efficiently. For the purposes of this research, information literacy is defined as the ability to access, evaluate, and use information from a variety of sources. At its most basic, it implies that individuals who are information literate are self-sufficient. The 1989 ALA Presidential Committee on Information Literacy's *Final Report* defined an information literate person as one,

> Who [has] learned how to learn . . . because they know how knowledge is organized, how to find information and how to use information in such a way that others can learn from them. They are people prepared for lifelong learning, because they can always find the information needed for any task or decision at hand. (ALA 1989)

The ALA's definition fails to realize that there is a set of problems between finding and using information; in a sense, an unaccounted for missing element. *A Progress Report on Information Literacy*, an update to the *Final Report*, was issued in March of 1998, outlining specific progress toward recommendations from the original report, as well as further recommendations. Among these is Recommendation 5, which is repeated from the *Final Report,* Recommendation 3:

> There needs to be more research and demonstration projects related to information literacy and its use—Progress: There are many significant directions that information literacy research needs to take. Among the most pressing research agendas are (1) how best to benchmark information literacy abilities and progress, (2) how to measure the effectiveness of information literacy programs on individual's performance, and (3) how information literacy is manifested in work settings and the degree to which it enhances workplace productivity. (Breivik, Hancock, and Senn 1998)

There are still no specific outcomes mentioned to address the previously identified missing elements.

While there is little consensus in the literature on the terminology (see Behrens 1994; Foster 1993; Mabandla 1996; McCrank 1991; Snavely and Cooper 1997; Strege 1997; White 1992), the concept of information literacy has been adopted and endorsed internationally (Booker 1992; Breivik 1992; Ford 1994; Moore 1997; Sayed and de Jager 1997; September 1993) by a large number of institutions of higher education including community colleges (Arp and Kenny 1990; Branch and Gilchrist 1996; Burns 1992; Metoyer-Duran 1992; SSCC[1] (1993); military education (Daragan and Stevens 1996); special libraries (Fisher and Bjorner 1994); the corporate environment (Hawes 1994); the K–12 environment (AASL[2] 1997; AASL and NCLIS[3] 1989; Breivik and Senn 1994); for accreditation purposes (MSACS[4] 1995; Swenson and Souter 1995); for instructing special populations (Dimitroff et al. 1990; Gilton 1994; Huston and Yribar 1991; Johnson-Cooper 1994); and other educational and professional organizations.

In 1992, Doyle reported in her dissertation findings on the results of a Delphi panel, a research technique "aimed at assisting a panel of experts reach a consensus on an issue through a reiterative and structured communications process" (p. 1). A group of 136 persons were invited to participate, and charged with developing a consensus on a definition of the term information literacy and naming outcome measures for the concept. Doyle provided an expanded definition of information literacy when she outlined the characteristics of an information literate person as one who:

1. recognizes that accurate and complete information is the basis for intelligent decision making;
2. recognizes the need for information;
3. formulates questions based on information needs;
4. identifies potential sources of information;
5. develops successful search strategies;
6. accesses sources of information including computer-based and other technologies;
7. evaluates information;
8. organizes information for practical application;
9. integrates new information into an existing body of knowledge; and
10. uses information in critical thinking and problem solving. (p. 2)

Doyle pointed out that this definition "highlights the process of information literacy" (p. 1), and continued:

> The attributes are potential rubrics for a checklist of skills comprising the process. This comprehensive definition is a valuable tool that goes beyond an explanatory function into an operational list of the desired outcomes. With these skills comes empowerment because the ability to use information is necessary to making informed decisions throughout a lifetime. (p. 1)

Bruce's 1996 doctoral dissertation and the subsequent published monograph based on the dissertation, *The Seven Faces of Information Literacy* (1997), proposed a relational model of information literacy as an alternative to the behavioral model that presently dominates information literacy education and research (Bruce 1997, p. i). Bruce's approach is at odds with Doyle's methodology and she outlined the comparison in her 1997 publication as follows:

BEHAVIORAL Doyle (1992)	RELATIONAL Bruce (1996, 1997)
derived from scholar's views	derived from user's experiences
derived from seeking consensus	derived from seeking variation
derived using the Delphi Technique	derived using phenomenography
recommends constructivist approaches to teaching and learning	recommends relational approaches to teaching and learning
sees information literacy as measurable	sees information literacy as not measurable
sees information literacy as definable	sees information literacy as describable
sees information literacy as quantifiable—asks how much has been learned?	sees information literacy as not quantifiable—asks what has been learned?
portrays information literacy in terms of attributes of persons	portrays information literacy in terms of conceptions, e.g. subject-object relations
focuses on personal qualities of the individual apart from the environment	focuses on personal qualities in relation to the environment

Figure 1.1. Doyle vs. Bruce. Adapted, by permission, from Bruce (1997), *The Seven Faces of Information Literacy,* p. 13.

The research presented in this book does not reject the relational view (Bruce 1996, 1997) in its entirety. It agrees with Bruce in that "many of these [Doyle's skills] statements are not easily assessed" (p. 70); however, it presumes that it is possible to construct a framework from which assessment can be accomplished.

Shapiro and Hughes (1996) questioned whether information literacy as a concept needs to be more widely construed. They also wondered if information literacy should be promoted and, if so, what should be accomplished by this. They continued and asked if information literacy should be,

> Something broader, something that enables individuals not only to use information and information technology effectively and adapt to their constant changes but also to think critically about the entire information enterprise and information society? Something more akin to a "liberal art"—knowledge that is part of what it means to be a free person in the present historical context of the dawn of the information age? (p. 32)

Shapiro and Hughes offered an information literacy curriculum that includes seven dimensions. The research presented in this book supports, in part, the seventh literacy—critical literacy—which they defined as "the ability to evaluate critically the intellectual, human and social strengths and weaknesses, potentials and limits, benefits and costs of information technologies" (p. 34).

The Nature of Information Literacy Literature

Most of the publications about information literacy in the library and information science and education literature alludes to the notion that many, if not most users, are lacking in information literacy skills. There is little evidence of empirical research on the subject of information literacy, yet, the literature reveals there is a large body of frequently cited discourse on this concept.

Breivik (1985, 1987, 1989, 1992), Breivik and Senn (1994), Bruce (1996, 1997), Doyle (1992, 1992a, 1994), Kuhlthau (1987, 1991), and Rader (1991, *Reference Services Review*), are well known for their discussions of information literacy, as well as other scholars and associations: American Association of School Librarians, ALA, Association of College and Research Libraries (ACRL), National Commission on Libraries and Information Science, *National Education Goals, Goals 2000: Educate America Act*, and the *SCANS Report*.[5] With the exception of Doyle (1992a) and Bruce's dissertation (1996), which explored information literacy theoretically, there is a marked lack of empirical research to substantiate what is basically a great deal of fragmented prescriptive and professional literature.

In particular, Kirk and Todd (1993) noted the fragmented nature of the limited information literacy research literature when they wrote "Available research is fragmented and piecemeal, without connection to prior research or sufficient concentration in one area to build a useful body of knowledge that can inform practice" (p. 129). Bruce (1997) confirmed this state of the literature and went on to list other notable features of the body of information literacy research as:

- the number of studies in this area is extremely limited, despite its perceived importance;
- available research outcomes have not led to any significant change in our understanding of information literacy;
- no studies have been located which focus on the views of people other than information literacy researchers and scholars or information professionals;

- researchers do not appear to be questioning existing understandings of information literacy despite confusion about the nature of information literacy and the questions raised by some scholars;
- researchers assume that information literacy is a transferable skill across discipline contexts and information problems; and,
- research studies have not been context specific, assuming instead the generic nature of information literacy before examining the phenomenon in specific contexts. (pp. 75-76)

The lack of reliable research in the literature is a critical factor when addressing the subject of information literacy. The information literacy literature is full of assumptions and generalizations, few of which are supported by empirical evidence. Eisenberg and Brown (1992) commented on the similar problem in the literature of library and information skills instruction. In discussing the four themes, the value of library skills instruction, the nature and scope of library and information skills, the integrated approach, and alternative methods of teaching library and information skills, the authors wrote:

These four themes represent understandings and assumptions that pervade the literature, state and local standards, and curricula, and guidelines for library [media] programs at all levels. Many seemingly excellent library and information skills instructional programs are built on them. Still the following critical and difficult questions must be asked:

Do we really know these themes to be accurate?
Is there hard evidence to confirm them?
Have they withstood careful scrutiny by researchers? (p. 103)

The research presented in this book addresses similar key and difficult questions about information literacy and the available literature. Specifically, in viewing the fragmented nature of the literature, and, attempting to characterize the literature, a number of questions are revealed.

Realistically and from a pragmatic point of view, what makes an individual information literate? What measurable and conceptual elements are involved in the development of an information literate individual? The ALA (1989) has introduced a theoretical definition, one that appears to be widely accepted and quoted as standard (see Daragon and Stevens 1996; Libutti 1991; Ochs et al. 1991; South Seattle Community College 1993). Doyle (1992) introduced ten individual skills, and Bruce (1996, 1997) suggested a relational model; however, these definitions are not practically based, nor do they provide answers to the questions relating to or for approaching information literacy systematically and empirically.

When the limited information literacy literature is reviewed and characterized systematically, along with the available library research and bibliographic instruction literature, with an eye toward assessable outcomes and conceptual elements, important questions, and key elements are identified. For the purposes of this study, these elements are identified as sociological and psychological factors and presumed to be correlated:

1. *Attitude*—How do students really feel about information literacy skills? The available literature is overwhelmingly skewed toward the perceptions of faculty and/or librarians (see Amstutz and Whitson 1997; Cannon 1994; Nowakowski and Frick 1995). With the exception of H. Morrison (1997), there is no other empirical evidence that provides information about how college-level students actually feel about these skills.

2. *Performance*—How do college-level students fare when tested or queried on information literacy skills? Hand in hand with attitudes about information literacy skills comes the students' actual performance when interpreting or performing these skills, whether it is represented in problem solving or information situations (see Geffert and Christensen 1998; Libutti 1991; Maughan 1994). The inclusion of this element balances the problem of self-reported data only (see Geffert and Bruce 1997).

3. *Relationship with faculty*—In terms of students becoming information literate as a result of the relationship between students and the faculty/advisor, what is the nature of this relationship between faculty and students? This factor surfaced repeatedly in the research and professional literature reviewed for this study, however, it was not identified as the relationship between the faculty/advisor and students. In the literature examined, the focus was on the importance of faculty and librarians working together to provide a learning, information skills environment through library resource-based instruction, and determining who is responsible for training students (see Amstutz and Whitson 1997; Arp and Wilson 1989; Cannon 1994; Lubans 1980; Thomas and Ensor 1982; Thomas 1994; Haws et al. 1989; Maynard 1990; Maio 1995; Nowakowski and Frick 1995).

4. *Exposure to* the library/information science environment—What has the student been exposed to in an information environment? *Merriam-Webster's Collegiate Online Dictionary* defines expose as "to submit or make accessible to a particular action or influ-

ence."[6] In this context, students must have the opportunity to be influenced by the library/information environment in some formalized manner (see Arp and Kenny 1990; Damko 1990; Farid et al.
1984; Geffert and Bruce 1997; Libutti 1991; Lowe 1995; Maughan
1994; Morner 1993; Parrish 1989a, 1989b; Thaxton 1985; Werrell
and Wesley 1990).

5. *Experience in* the library/information environment—What is the
   students experience in an information environment? If a student is
   to become information literate in an environment that more and
   more is dependent on information as economy, he or she must be
   able to demonstrate evidence of knowledge acquired (experience)
   during the exposure. Examples of experience include knowledge of
   bibliographic style, publication cycles of published literature, database selection, and scope of topic (see Compton 1989; Farid et al.
   1984; Hernandez 1985; Libutti 1991; Morner 1993; Ochs et al.
   1991; Osiobe 1988; B. Park 1986a; Reed 1974; Thaxton 1985;
   Watkins 1973; York et al. 1988).

The research presented in this book is driven in part by these sociological and psychological factors. It also focuses on the skill of evaluation within Doyle's (1992) set of information literacy skills. For the
purposes of this research, the skill of evaluation is regarded as the crucial element of the process generally known as information literacy
because the ability to recognize the relevancy, currency, reliability,
completeness, and accuracy of information comes from personal
knowledge and experience. It should also be noted that this skill is the
one that college-level students have identified as the one with which
they are the least confident (Morner 1993; H. Morrison 1997). This is
also the only evidence that the ten skills may not be equal.

In viewing Doyle's (1992) ten skills there is evidence that simple
searches for known information can be completed successfully, satisfy-
ing 50 percent of the ten Doyle information literacy skills. At the time
of this study, however, there had been no research to determine if the
claims that many college-level students were not information literate
were in fact true and, if so, to what extent and how to combat it. There
was also no empirical evidence to determine the components, if any, of
the information literacy skills process. Doyle's ten skills represent outcomes. A person is considered information literate if they master the
competencies outlined in the ten skills; however, the skills themselves
are not sufficient to evaluate this process. There has been only one attempt to determine college-level students' attitudes about information
literacy—to determine if they view the separate characteristics of an
information literate individual differently (H. Morrison 1997). In this

research, H. Morrison reported that the characteristic of evaluating information was unanimously agreed upon by the participants as the most advanced (p. 7).

The published literature reveals little empirical evidence of research conducted on the separate information literacy skills. With the exception of Morner (1993) and Maughan (1994), little evidence exists on the evaluation skills of college-level students, particularly in view of the explosion of information and scholarly published literature. When one views information literacy skills individually, the resulting picture is fragmented. Individual information literacy skills have been broadly addressed and assessed in the aggregate. In viewing the literature, these skills can be found by examining the documents and materials produced by using keywords and subjects such as bibliographic instruction, information literacy, information skills, information competencies, and library instruction. This also makes it difficult to generalize any findings, or characterize the literature in any logical way, and there is little, if any, standardization.

Purpose of Study

This study was undertaken to:

- investigate the sociological and psychological factors, as evidenced in the literature, that are believed to affect college-level students' ability to make relevance judgments;
- determine the extent of the relationship between sociological and psychological factors in the information literacy framework;
- collect information about the attitudes of college-level students toward Doyle's (1992) ten information literacy skills; and,
- identify college-level students' attitudes and perceptions about previously identified relevance/evaluative criteria.

In order to achieve this purpose the study adapted and administered the Morner Test of Library Research Skills developed and validated by Morner in her 1993 dissertation, *A Test of Library Research Skills for Education Doctoral Students*.

Research Questions and Hypotheses

The research in this book investigated the following research questions and hypotheses.

Research Questions

1. What are the sociological and psychological factors that affect information literacy skills?
2. What is the extent of the relationship between sociological and psychological factors in the information literacy framework?
3. What are the attitudes and perceptions of college-level students about Doyle's (1992) ten information literacy skills?
4. What are the attitudes and perceptions of college-level students about pre-identified relevance/evaluative criteria?

Hypotheses

1. If the attitudinal component of information literacy skills is high, then the performance component will be high.
2. If the level of exposure in a college-level student is found to be high, then the measure of the performance component of information literacy skills will be high.
3. If the level of experience in a college-level student is found to be high, then the measure of the performance component of information literacy skills will be high.
4. If the strength of the relationship between students and faculty is found to be high, then the measure of the performance component of information literacy skills will be high.
5. If the level of exposure is found to be high in college-level students, then the measure of the attitudinal component of information literacy skills will be high.
6. If the level of experience is found to be high in college-level students, then the measure of the attitudinal component of information literacy skills will be high.
7. If the strength of the relationship between students and faculty is found to be high, then the measure of the attitudinal component of information literacy skills will be high.

Definition of Terms

The following definitions will be used for this study.

1. *Information literacy*—the ability to access, evaluate, and use information from a variety of sources.
2. *Information literate*—a person that is able to recognize when information is needed and has the ability to locate, evaluate, and use effectively the needed information. This person has

learned how to learn because they know how knowledge is organized, how to find information and how to use information in such a way that others can learn from them (ALA 1989).

3. *Literacy*—the ability to read and write; also, the ability to find and evaluate needed information so that the reader can function and work as a productive member of society.

4. *Relevance*—the user's perceptions about the potential of certain information to resolve his or her problems in the context of his or her information seeking and use situations (Schamber and Bateman 1996).

5. *Relevance judgments*—the users' decisions to accept or reject specific information items based on subject and situational criteria (adapted from Schamber and Bateman 1996).

6. *Evaluation*—the ability to analyze critically information and resources for use in information problem solving.

7. *Relationship with faculty*—the nature of the relationship between the student (advisee) and the faculty (advisor) for graduate students; and, for undergraduate students, this encompasses the nature of the relationship between the instructor/professor and student in the classroom environment.

8. *Exposure*—the amount of exposure to an information literacy skills environment (e.g., library orientation, bibliographic instruction, for credit course).

9. *Experience*—the amount of experience a student has in using information literacy skills (e.g., knowledge of bibliographic style, publication cycles of published literature, database selection, scope of topic).

10. *Performance*—the level of students' knowledge when tested for evaluation skills as is evidenced in responses to specific queries.

11. *Attitude*—the students' attitude/comfort level toward the ten information literacy skills as characterized by Doyle (1992).

Methodology

This study surveyed undergraduate, master's and doctoral students enrolled in required core curriculum courses in all majors in the School of Education, College of Applied Human Sciences, at a land-grant Carnegie Class I research institution in the western portion of the United States (Targeted University). The undergraduate program is the educator licensing program; the two master's programs are the master of science degree in student affairs in higher education, and the master of science degree in education and human resource studies (six specializations); and the doctor of philosophy degree in education and human resource studies has seven program specializations.

Entire classes were randomly selected from the Targeted University's fall 1998 class schedule in accordance with the Human Research Guidelines at the Targeted University and the Institutional Review Board at the University of Pittsburgh.

A preliminary review of the data collected as of January 19, 1999, and the beginning of the spring 1999 semester revealed a majority of master's respondents, a few doctoral students, seventeen seniors, and one junior. In order to increase the diversity of the sample, an ethnic studies course (ET200) comprised mostly of undergraduates was tested. This course counts as the required diversity component for the School of Education. After testing this population, the undergraduate population was more diverse including twenty-five seniors, seventeen juniors, sixteen sophomores, and five freshmen.

Pilot Study

Since this was a new model based on an adapted survey instrument, to correct any errors in comprehension and readability, and to determine the amount of time needed to complete the test, feedback on the initial version of the instrument was collected from a group of students who represented the undergraduate, master's, and doctoral levels in the School of Education at the Targeted University. The instrument was reviewed by a representative from the Office of Budgets/Institutional Analysis at the Targeted University, and recommended changes for clarifying ambiguous items, and in general, making items more clear, were made before soliciting feedback from students. The chairs of the three department levels (undergraduate, master's, doctoral) in the School of Education assisted in identifying one class per department from which to solicit feedback. The results of the feedback sessions assisted in the refining of the survey instrument.

Instrumentation

An automated survey instrument was used to collect the data. (Neely, 2000, pp. 247-79). The survey instrument was adapted from the instrument developed and validated by Morner in her 1993 dissertation. The Morner Test of Library Research Skills (Morner Test) is an instrument designed to measure the library research skills of doctoral education students. The resulting instrument was named The Neely Test of Relevance, Evaluation, and Information Literacy Attitudes (Neely Test).

For the present study, some survey items were changed and others added to allow for more variability, the addition of undergraduate and masters level students as test subjects, and to conform to the model developed for this study (see chapter 3, figure 3.2, p. 38). The model developed is a variance sensitive model which requires items to be variance generative.

An acknowledged weakness of Morner's instrument is the small number of items (n=5) in each content cluster area. Another weakness relevant to this study is that the instrument was developed for doctoral students only, so it was necessary to include additional explanatory items for the benefit of undergraduate and master's level students. This research study is concerned with attitudes about information literacy skills, and Morner's instrument does not directly address information literacy. In her review of the literature section, as well as in her preliminary qualitative research, Morner noted the importance of the relationship with faculty; however, no allowance was made for this area in her instrument. The current study required the development of a specific model that includes the following variables: exposure, relationship with faculty, experience, attitude, performance, and relevance. There is also a section for gathering demographic data. Detailed survey item development is included in the dissertation on which this book is based (Neely 2000).

Data Analysis

In addition to descriptive statistical analysis and regression analysis, correlations between subscales or indices (elements), and groups (males and females; undergraduates and graduates), and T-tests were performed to test the model (see chapter 3, figure 3.2, p. 38). Data will be described using descriptive statistics which includes percentages, means, and graphical representations. In order to test the model, an index score was determined for individual test items, elements of the model, and group of individuals based on the survey instrument. As a result of the way some of the survey questions are constructed and the type of answer being elicited, all data gathered was not used to test the model. Based on the premise that the most heavily weighted items are the ones with the most positive values, a method was developed to determine index scores. A complete discussion of how each item is weighted appears in the dissertation on which this book is based (Neely 2000).

Notes

1. South Seattle Community College (SSCC).
2. American Association of School Librarians (AASL).
3. National Commission on Libraries and Information Science (NCLIS).
4. Middle States Association of Colleges and Schools (MSACS).
5. Goals 2000: Educate America Act, Title III, Sec. 302 became law in 1994, amended in 1996. [On-line]. See http://www.ed.gov/legislation/GOALS2000/ TheAct/. *The Secretary's Commission on Achieving Necessary Skills* (1991). *What Work Requires of Schools: A SCANS Report for America 2000*. Washington, D.C.: U.S. Department of Labor, Government Printing Office.
6. Merriam-Webster Language Center. [On-line]. See http://www.m-w.com/home.htm (accessed 21 December 2001).

Chapter 2

The Information Literacy Framework

The framework developed for this study is derived from the research and professional literature. In addition to the sociological and psychological factors identified previously—exposure, experience, relationship with faculty, performance, and attitude—are evaluation, the growth of scholarly communication, information anxiety, and overload. These are all an integral part of this theoretical approach to information literacy.

The skill of evaluation is but one of the ten aforementioned characteristics of an information literate individual. There is little evidence in the literature to suggest these ten skills are of equal value. In fact, H. Morrison's (1997) research, which found that of the four skills (recognizing a need for information, locating information, evaluating information, and effectively using information), evaluating information was unanimously voted the most advanced skill (p. 7), is the only evidence, using the Doyle (1992) characteristics, of the skills being weighted differently. Findings from Morner (1993) include items on evaluating as well as other areas. However, the ten skills themselves have not been specifically assessed as a whole and, thus, have not been weighted.

In viewing the ten, it appears that some are necessary in order to complete some tasks; for example, to use and interpret the results of an on-line catalog search. An author search ["a = Neely"] would result in an alphabetical list of authors beginning with "Neely, A" as shown in figure 2.1, section 1. If the known author's first name begins with the letter "C," the user would select line no. 2 (in **bold**). The results of this action are illustrated in figure 2.1, section 2.

| *Search Request: A=NEELY* | *University of Pittsburgh* | **Section 1** |
| *Search Results: 83 Entries Found* | *Author Guide* | |

LINE: BEGINNING ENTRY:
INDEX RANGE:
1 NEELY ALFRED S.   ETHICS IN GOVERNMENT LAWS ARE THEY TOO ETH   1 - 14
2 **NEELY BRAXTEL L.**   **MAGNITUDE AND FREQUENCY OF FLOODS IN ARKA**   **15 - 28**
3 NEELY FRANK HENRY 1884. RICHS A SOUTHERN INSTITUTION SINCE   29 - 42
4 NEELY JOHN 1920.   PRACTICAL METALLURGY AND MATERIALS OF IND   43 - 56

| *Search Request: A=NEELY* | *University of Pittsburgh* | **Section 2.**[1] |
| **Search Results: 83 Entries Found** | **Author Index** | |

NEELY BRAXTEL L.
17 TWO DIMENSIONAL RELAXATION METHOD FLOW MODEL <1992> (C1)
18 TWO DIMENSIONAL RELAXATION METHOD FLOW MODEL <1992> (J1)
19 WATER SURFACE PROFILES ALONG BAYOU METO AND <1985> microfiche (C1)
NEELY BROCK WESLEY
20 *Search Under: NEELY W BROCK WESLEY BROCK 1926
NEELY CAROL THOMAS 1939
21 BROKEN NUPTIALS IN SHAKESPEARES PLAYS <1985> (C1)
22 BROKEN NUPTIALS IN SHAKESPEARES PLAYS <1985> (G1)
23 WOMANS PART FEMINIST CRITICISM OF SHAKESPEARE <1980> (C1)

Figure 2.1. Known author search in University of Pittsburgh on-line catalog.

A known title search, depending on whether or not the library owns the item and on the on-line system, would provide you with one of two results, as shown in figures 2.2 and 2.3.

Search Request: **T=BROKEN NUPTIALS IN SHAKESPEARES PLA**
                                                    University of Pittsburgh
BOOK-Record 1 of 2 Entries Found   -------------*Long View*

TITLE: Broken nuptials in Shakespeare's plays / Carol Thomas Neely.
AUTHOR: Neely, Carol Thomas, 1939-
PUBLISHED: New Haven : Yale University Press, c1985.
DESCRIPTION: xi, 261 p. ; 22 cm.
ISBN: 0300033419
NOTES: Includes index.
          Bibliography: p. 211-253.
SUBJECTS (LIBRARY OF CONGRESS): (use s= search)
          Shakespeare, William, 1564-1616--Characters--Women.
          Shakespeare, William, 1564-1616--Knowledge--Manners and
             customs.
          Marriage in literature.
          Women in literature.

Figure 2.2. Known title search in University of Pittsburgh on-line catalog where title is owned.

Search Request: T=ME AND MY SHADOW   *University of Pittsburgh*
Search Results: 0 Entries Found   *No Title Entries Found*

                    No Title Entries Found

Possible reasons for this message are:

   * *Title may not be in this database.*
   * *Initial articles were used. EXAMPLES: a, an, the, le, el, der.*
   * *Title was typed incorrectly.*

Tips:

   * *Omit initial article. EXAMPLES: a, an, the, le, el, der.*
   * *Check spelling or shorten the title.*
   * *Remove all punctuation.*
   * *Try searching by keyword.*
For more information on TITLE SEARCHING, type explain t

Figure 2.3. Known title search in University of Pittsburgh on-line catalog where title is not owned.

In cases where the specific author/title is not known, the knowledge alone—of being able to complete this process—is not sufficient. If these types of searches (known author/title) are successful and result in the desired item, they could be considered, at least by the user, as successful search strategies (Information literacy skill #5). The user has thus recognized an information need (Information literacy skill #2); formulated a request based on this need (Information literacy skill #3) (I want a book by Carol Neely/I want to find *Broken Nuptials in Shakespeare's Plays*/ I want to find *Me and My Shadow*); identified potential sources of information (Information literacy skill #4) (the library's online catalog); and accessed a computer-based source of information (Information literacy skill #6). In this instance, the user has satisfied five of the ten information literacy characteristics; but does this make the user information literate?

The skill of evaluation is a critical one in the information literacy framework. How well or how poorly users make relevance judgments in evaluating information for use and problem solving is related to the other information literacy skills; however, the literature provides no clues as to the nature of this relationship. Hayden recognized the critical mass that the proliferation of information has reached in society in general when she wrote,

> The information entering our world each day is composed of facts, data, figures, details, tidbits, advice, wisdom and even lore. By itself, information is not knowledge. Information and data must be gathered, read, assembled, observed, questioned, conceptualized, judged, manipulated, integrated, analyzed, synthesized, and evaluated before it becomes knowledge. Information must be filtered through our experiences and applied to our lives in order to become knowledge. It must be used and reflected upon to become meaningful, otherwise it remains just facts and figures.

The Growth of Scholarly Communication

It has been estimated that the body of information quadruples every five years (Tiefel 1993, p. 57), with more than 100 million publications from the U.S. Federal Government each year (Biden 1997, p. 125). Along with the enormous volume, we must consider the complexity of the information that is being produced. This growing complexity has been a continual problem for many years, for the subject expert as well as the novice. For example, in his well known and often quoted 1945 article "As We May Think," Bush remarked on the "growing mountain of research," (p. 101) and the increasing problems that necessary specialization has created. He noted that "specialization becomes increasingly necessary for progress. . . . The investigator [researcher] is staggered by the findings and conclusions of thousands of other workers—conclusions which he cannot find time to grasp, much less to remember, as they appear" (p. 101).

Today, it seems reasonable to presume that the researchers, even subject experts, are experiencing greater difficulty. There appear to be at least several reasons for this increasing difficulty: the volume of information, the complexity of the information, and greater accessibility. In as much as the volume of information is increasing exponentially, access to this information has increased as well. Tiefel (1993) argued that "the proliferation of information has intensified the need for students to be able to evaluate information" (p. 57). She continued,

> The challenge often lies not in being able to find enough information but in being able to select the most useful information for meeting their specific needs. Thus, two instructional needs in "information-seeking skills" must be satisfied: To teach students how to find needed information, using whatever formats are most efficient; and then to evaluate that information in order to select what is most appropriate to the task at hand. (p. 57)

Given this state of affairs, it appears as if information literacy skills one through six can adequately be completed and/or accomplished, with some degree of success. Automation and increasingly user-friendly search engines and interfaces make it possible to retrieve "something" in a keyword search in almost any database, on-line catalogs, and the Internet. Searches could not be so easily accomplished nor would they yield a similar volume of results if they were conducted manually, using only print-based resources.

A focus group study (H. Morrison 1997) of the attitudes of undergraduates at Concordia University College of Alberta, Canada, toward information literacy skills revealed the participants disagreed on whether or not the recognition of the need for information (Information literacy skill #2) was a skill. This same group agreed unanimously that locating information was "particularly challenging today because of the abundance of sources," and identified the relationship between the attitudes of the information seeker and locating information (p. 7).

Bush (1945) noted, "The difficulty seems to be, not so much that we publish unduly in view of the extent and variety of present-day interests, but rather that publication has been extended far beyond our present ability to make real use of the record" (p. 102). Reeves (1996) contends that "one of the major obstacles to the creative and systemic transformation of the learning experience, and thus to the competitiveness of the U.S., is the problem of information and complexity" (p. xv). He continued in this vein by noting that the "true literacy bar," which includes "a variety of thinking skills," has been raised, and yet, the programs aimed at meeting the minimum, and at dealing with the complexity of information, still retain vestiges of old literacy skills (p. xi). He noted that increasing reading abilities and memory enhancement programs also do not deal with the problems of complexity "that require skills of filtering, organization, and reflection" (p. xi). Reeves also believed that the lives of students, teachers, workers, and business managers have a common factor, "the increasing and debilitating complexity of their world due to the explosion of data, information, and knowledge" (p. xv).

Information Anxiety and Information Overload

It appears that along with the growth and complexity of information, the concerns of the "experts" have increased as well. Information overload is an acute issue in this regard, and J. Rudd and M. J. Rudd (1986a, 1986b), Mellon (1986), and Keefer (1993) have provided insight into how college-level students cope with information overload and information anxiety. It is difficult to sift relevant information from the overwhelming volume being published. The search for the "key" article instead of the merely relevant one is an important quest for information seekers in all disciplines.

The information problems faced by experts and novices alike are compounded by the increasing volume and complexity of published material, and increased accessibility due to technology, which lead to feelings of information overload and information anxiety explained by Wurman (1989) as occurring when one:

- does not understand available information;
- feels overwhelmed by the amount of information to be understood;
- does not know if certain information exists;
- does not know where to find information;
- knows where to find information, but does not have the key to access it. (p. 44)

For the purposes of this discussion, the author concedes that there is a wealth of information that even the experts in their specific fields are unable to adequately deal with, especially when they step outside the realm of their specializations. Also, the author concedes that making a request for a specific item, whether via an intermediary (individual) or via a machine (information retrieval), requires little creativity or imagination. However, the problem arises when said user is given an array of choices. This occurs, for example, when one makes an information request and receives back numerous choices. Is this user, expert or novice, equipped with the appropriate evaluative skills to make these relevance judgments? Meadow (1992) simplified our understanding of the information retrieval process when he wrote,

> Information retrieval is a communication process. It involves an author, composer, artist, or other record originator and a reader, viewer, listener, or user of information. But these two principles are not in direct communication. A record is created for *later* use. And its use requires finding the record among large numbers of other records, all of which share some attributes that caused them to be grouped together in the first place. In addition, there are others who may be directly or indirectly involved: those who decide what aspects of a record should be represented in the computer-searchable database; those who transform, index, or encode the information in various ways to create the computer record; those who help the user perform the search; those who design and implement the computer software; and those who decide what services will be offered to users. (p. xvii)

When viewed in this regard, is it a fair assumption that the average college-level student or novice is not prepared to use this information effectively or efficiently? Is it also unlikely that he or she possesses more than a few of the information literacy skills?

Note

---

1. Searches illustrated in figures 2.1, 2.2, and 2.3 were conducted in 1997, before the University of Pittsburgh acquired a windows-based on-line library catalog.

Chapter 3

Evaluation, Relevance, and Information Literacy: A Bibliographic Essay

The purpose of this chapter is to review the research and professional literature relevant to this study. This review of the literature is based on the model developed for this study (see figure 3.2). The research and professional literature presented here is derived from the education, library science, and information science fields. This discussion includes the concept of evaluation and a historical perspective of the evolution of the concept of relevance. The model developed, which depicts the relationship of relevance to information literacy, is introduced and the research and professional literature is examined based on the elements of the model—exposure, experience, relationship with faculty, performance, and attitude.

This bibliographical essay reviews the major elements of the study, based on the model, and identifies, reviews, and presents the key papers that support those elements. Additional supporting literature will be referenced but not fully explored. A complete discussion of the review of all of the relevant research and professional literature supporting this study can be found in the original dissertation upon which this study is based (Neely 2000, pp. 56-110).

Evaluation

Evaluation is a human process that relies upon a combination of personal skills and knowledge. Users must be able to critically evaluate all information by questioning and making judgments about the value, type, purpose, scope, and use of the information. For electronic databases and Internet sources, similar evaluative judgments must be made.

The library science literature on the skill of evaluation is fairly limited and focused on library science education. W. A. Katz's *Introduction to Reference Work* (1992, 1997), and Bopp and Smith's *Reference and Information Services* (1995) remain the leading texts which provide the basics on evaluating information for acquisition and collection development by librarians and information providers. W. A. Katz notes, in the sixth edition, that "while written primarily for students of reference service and practicing reference librarians, the book is an introduction to basic sources that can also help laypeople [*sic*] use the library effectively" (1992, p. xv).

Librarians have developed a set of general criteria for evaluating information resources. These criteria, designed for professional librarians and commonly referred to in library education, are general enough to be applied more broadly, in a variety of ways. The following concepts about evaluating resources are taken from the W. A. Katz text.

1. *Purpose*—the purpose of the resource in relation to the information need; should be evident from the title or form; Evaluative question—Has the author or compiler fulfilled the purpose?
2. *Authority*—the credentials of the author, editor, or compiler, and publisher; personal understanding and depth of knowledge and subject; objectivity and fairness of work.
3. *Scope*—is this piece of information the appropriate one for the information need?
4. *Cost*—a factor for users in searching fee-based online databases, and in some cases, interlibrary loan and document delivery.
5. *Format*—arrangement of resource; ease of use; currency, intended audience; cross reference and indexes (print); simple classification; clear and current photographs, charts, tables and diagrams; often the format (print, non-print, microfiche) of a resource is a concern in the information seeking process. Users may erroneously believe the computer database includes everything and neglect print-based sources which are just as important. (pp. 25-29)

W. A. Katz also points out that it is more important to evaluate data-bases than print versions because of the lack of standardization among different databases. Other areas specific to databases include various formats for storage, accessibility, how is resource updated and how often, and hardware and software specifications (1992, 23-29; 1997, 25-29).

Without the experience and knowledge of the evaluation process, users cannot be expected to make informed decisions based on the abundance of information available. Ultimately, it is the outcome of this process that allows the other information literacy skills to be ac-complished. In a 1998 article outlining the development of an informa-tion literacy program (ILP) at the University of Maine at Farmington, Furlong and Roberts confirm that "Articulating this need to evaluate is at the heart of the ILP" (para. 17).

Research on evaluation and evaluative skills is even more limited and discouraging. There are no studies which address evaluation solely. Empirical evidence from recent studies (Morner 1993; H. Morrison 1997) reveals that scores on items on evaluation and relevance were not as high as the other information literacy and library skills tested. Mor-ner, in her preliminary qualitative research, and H. Morrison, in her exploratory research, interviewed students and found that evaluation of resources and information was a critical skill with which they had the least amount of confidence. Morner's dissertation, which developed a test of library research skills for education doctoral students, identified and established eight content clusters including one on evaluating in-formation resources. An analysis of the five test items identified by Morner as falling in that content cluster showed that only 25 percent of those queried (n=149) knew which source was least likely to aid in evaluating the credentials of an author, and only 32 percent knew that an article could be evaluated for bias, and how to evaluate it, before actually reading it. It is often assumed that once students reach the graduate level they are "automatically" equipped with the appropriate skills to conduct original research. Morner's findings confirm what library and information professionals have believed, that this is not always the case (see also Dreifuss 1981; Parrish 1989a; Zaporozhetz 1987).

Relevance

There is a significant body of the information science relevance litera-ture that has implications for the skill of evaluation in the information literacy framework. Schamber's "Relevance and Information Behavior" (1994), and Saracevic's "Relevance Reconsidered" (1996) both provide in depth discussions of the various views or frameworks of relevance, which include:

1. *Systems relevance*—a direct match between query terms and document terms within a system; relies on phenomena such as document terms and exact or partial term-matching logics; represents points 8 and 9 on the information retrieval (IR) model (see figure 3.1). Common terms—matching, similarity (Belkin and Croft 1987; Salton 1992); system relevance response (King and Bryant 1971); and topicality (Barry 1994; Schamber, Eisenberg, and Nilan 1990).

2. *Information relevance*—a human judgment (subjective) of conceptual relatedness between a request and a document; judgment dependent on the internal knowledge of the judge; represents points 3 and 4, and 8 and 9 in figure 3.1). Common terms—aboutness (Ingwersen 1992); relevance (Kemp 1974; Lancaster and Warner 1993; Saracevic, Kantor, Chamis, and Trivison 1988); and topicality (Cool, Belkin, Frieder, and Kantor 1993; Wang 1994); and logical relevance (W. S. Cooper 1971).

3. *Situation relevance*—a relationship between information and the user's information problem situation; assumes only users can make valid judgments concerning the potential ability of information to solve their problems. Common terms—relevance and usefulness (Rees and Schultz 1967); relevance and utility (Saracevic et al. 1988); relevance and satisfaction (Tessier, Crouch, and Atherton 1977); and topicality and relevance (Cool et al. 1993). Following W. S. Cooper's (1971) concept of logical relevance comes situational relevance (Wilson 1973); relevance in a broad sense (Harter 1992; Schamber et al. 1990); intuitive use (Saracevic 1975; Schamber 1994, 6-8). Saracevic (1996) continues and adds

4. *Communication relevance*—relevance is considered as the criterion for establishing effectiveness of communication between a source and a destination (Saracevic 1975).

5. *Psychological relevance*—emphasis is on cognition; relevance deals with maximization of communication and cognition; is viewed as a dynamic, ever changing interpretation of information need in relation to presented texts (Harter 1992).

6. *Interaction*—information retrieval has evolved into a highly interactive process since the introduction of on-line systems during the 1970s.

Although none of these models has been widely adopted so far, Saracevic noted two stand out: cognitive model (Ingwersen 1992,

1996)—IR interaction is viewed as a set of processes of cognitive representations and modeling occurring and between the evolved elements; and episode model (Belkin, Cool, Stein, and Thiel 1995)— interaction is viewed as a sequence of episodes of different kinds (Saracevic 1996, 6-9).

This discussion of relevance is concerned primarily with the situation view; however, it is important in any discussion of relevance, as Schamber (1994) notes, to define "the context in which information scientists understand and apply the concept" (p. 5). Figure 3.1 is duplicated from Schamber's review titled "Relevance and Information Behavior" in the 1994 issue of the *Annual Review of Information Science and Technology*.

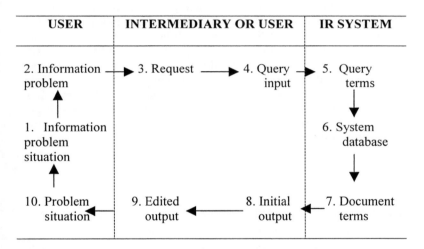

Figure 3.1. IR Interaction Model. Duplicated with permission from L. Schamber, whose figure appeared in "Relevance and Information Behavior," 1994, *Annual Review of Information Science and Technology*, p. 5.

Schamber noted that "The model illustrates points at which relationships can be evaluated between tangible representations of the user's problem . . . and representations of the information . . . human relevance judgments are collected at points 8 and 9" (p. 5). Schamber summarized the assumptions made about relevance and human judgment perspectives (Harter 1992; Saracevic 1970, 1975; Schamber et al. 1990) into the following:

1. Subjective, depending on human (user or nonuser) judgment and thus not an inherent characteristic of information or a document;
2. Cognitive, depending ultimately on human knowledge and perceptions;
3. Situational, relating to individual users' information problems;
4. Multidimensional, influenced by many factors;
5. Dynamic, constantly changing over time; and
6. Measurable, observable at a single point in time. (p. 6)

There are several excellent published reviews of the relevance literature by Saracevic including "The Concept of 'Relevance' in Information Science: A Historical Review" (1970), "Relevance: A Review of and a Framework for Thinking in Notion in Information Science" (1975), and "Relevance Reconsidered 1996" (1996). In 1994 Schamber's "Relevance and Information Behavior" was published; and in 1990, Schamber along with Eisenberg and Nilan published "A Reexamination of Relevance: Toward a Dynamic, Situational Definition." Schamber et al. reported that the concept of relevance had been a significant part of information retrieval research since the late 1950s when the International Conference for Scientific Information (ICSI) was held. At that time, Vickery's "The Structure of Information Retrieval Systems" (1959a), and "Subject Analysis for Information Retrieval" (1959b) noted that arguments about relevance revolved around two broad areas: relevance to a subject (topical or system) and relevance to a user.

Defining Relevance

The following sections will introduce the various definitions and concepts associated with relevance as it has developed in the information science literature. Topical-based or system relevance is the definition most commonly associated with information retrieval systems. It will also introduce specific empirical based criterion that have been elicited directly from users in information evaluation situations. User-based relevance and its development in the literature is discussed in the last section.

Topical-Based or System Relevance

The most widely accepted definition of relevance in terms of the topic and query matching the topic of the document is one of what Schamber et al. call the "best match" principal, or topicality, or what Saracevic (1970) identified as the systems view of information retrieval. Schamber et al. pointed out that much attention has been paid to this definition because it "may be that improving topical relevance has seemed both a logical and manageable first step toward achieving effective information retrieval" (p. 758). In a special topics issue of the *Journal of the American Society of Information Science* (*JASIS*), Froehlich (1994) and T. K. Park (1994) agreed that "most of the traditional work on relevance judgments has focused on the topicality of information retrieval systems." In that same issue, Barry (1994) pointed out the assumptions that would have to be accepted in order to prescribe to the topical approach of relevance as a criterion in evaluating the effectiveness of systems:

1. the subject terms used in the query can adequately describe a user's information need situation;
2. the subject terms assigned to a document can adequately describe the content of the document; and
3. subject matching results in the retrieval of relevant documents. (p. 150)

Barry (1994), Hersh (1994), Janes (1994), Sutton (1994), all contributors to the 1994 *JASIS* issue on relevance, and Schamber et. al either rejected this definition of topicality or agreed that this definition alone is insufficient. T. K. Park (1994) concluded

Topical relevance is context-free and is based on fixed assumptions about the relationship between a topic of a document and a search question, ignoring an individuals particular context and state of needs. It is an uni-dimensional view of users' information problems, disregarding the changing nature of the individual's information problem and its subsequent impact on the search. It fails to focus on the complexity of the individual's background and task situation. (p. 136)

User-Based Relevance and User-Based Relevance Criteria

There is a wealth of professional literature that is available on relevance which emphasizes the subjective aspects of relevance judgments. The following writers have discussed and/or suggested factors other than topicality upon which users' judgments can be based. Many of these authors also report on user-based criteria derived empirically or based on deductive logic. User-based relevance criterion are the characteristics used by users to evaluate information or to make relevance judgments.

"The Relevance of Relevance to the Testing and Evaluation of Document Retrieval Systems" (Rees 1966) criticizes evaluations of information retrieval systems that involve judges who do not originate the question and characterizes relevance judgments as "the expression of the user's opinion as to how the information conveyed by a document matches, overlaps, complements and/or is useful to his conceptual framework or previous knowledge" (pp. 318, 322). Rees believed that in designing and evaluating information retrieval systems, the behavior of the user as "generator, requestor, and ultimate processor of information" must be taken into account (p. 323).

Rees identified restrictions other than subject matter that influenced judgments of relevance as: the user's personality, education, and experience; the purpose for which information is being sought; the environment in which judgments are being made; and the point in time at which the judgment is made, in relation to the work at hand (p. 322).

W. S. Cooper's "A Definition of Relevance for Information Retrieval" (1971) developed the notion of logical relevance where a relevant document is one that contains at least one statement that is relevant to the question. This definition depends on the concept of logical consequence. He wanted "to define relevance as a relationship holding between pieces of stored information on the one hand and user's information needs formulated as information need representations on the other hand" (p. 22). Later in "On Selecting a Measure of Retrieval Effectiveness" (1973), and "Indexing Documents by Gendanken Experimentation" (1978), he viewed relevance as "has to do with aboutness" (or pertinence or topical-appropriateness); and noted that utility was an umbrella-like concept that involved "topic-relatedness, quality, importance, credibility;" a term for "anything about a document a user values" (subject matter, aesthetics, entertainment value) (1973, p. 92).

Cooper's (1971, 1973, 1978) factors which might influence a requester's judgments of utility include the information already in the requester's memory; the requester's background; the ease with which relevance can be detected by the requester to understand the information; the "quality" of a document; the document's importance or popularity; the urgency of the need for information; and the cost involved in obtaining information.

Foskett's "A Note on the Concept of 'Relevance'" (1972) advocated resurrecting the term pertinence and noted that relevance should be defined as "belonging to the field/subject/universe of discourse delimited by the terms of the request, as established by workers in that field"; and pertinence should be seen as "adding new information to the store already in the mind of the user, which is useful to him in the work that prompted the request" (p. 77). He believed that the relevance of a particular document to a particular request was something which could be agreed upon by several people who were experts in the field, and the pertinence of a particular document to a particular need could only be decided by the person with the need (p. 77).

In 1973, Wilson's "Situational Relevance" introduced the concept of situational relevance based on W. S. Cooper's (1971) definition of logical relevance. "Situationally relevant items are those that answer, or logically help to answer, questions of concern" (p. 457). He defines situational relevance as "relevance to a particular individual's situation—but to the situation as he sees it, not as others see it or as it 'really' is" (p. 460).

In "Relevance, Pertinence and Information System Development" (1974), Kemp discussed pertinence and factors that affect relevance such as the novelty of documents to requesters; the availability of documents and information; ease of access to information; the textual language and form of presentation; the requester's education and experiential background; and the requester's prior knowledge about the subject area (pp. 44-45).

In Maron's "On Indexing, Retrieval and the Meaning of About" (1977), the subject content of a document is what the document is about and is "the very heart of the indexing procedure" (p. 39). He distinguished between the aboutness of subject content (objective about—"the [actual or potential] behavior of asking or searching for writings"), and subjective about which "is the relationship between a document and the resulting inner experience of readers" (p. 41).

Maron defined aboutness as a key ingredient for the satisfaction of users' information needs. Other factors include comprehensibility, credibility, degree of importance, timeliness, and style (p. 42).

Swanson distinguished between objective relevance (written request becomes independent of its creator [p. 391]; objective relevance must meet standards of criticism in order to be accepted [p. 392]); and subjective relevance (requesters judgment of relevance) (p. 390) in "Some Unexplained Aspects of the Cranfield Tests of Indexing Performance Factors" (1986). He defined the relevance of a document as a piece of new knowledge, constructed by the requester in light of some information need. A document is relevant to a request if the requester says it is relevant. He noted that at that time, the implications of this idea had not been sufficiently explored. In later publications, Swanson (1986, 1988) described only two factors other than topicality that might have influenced the requester's judgments of relevance: requester's own knowledge and background; and all other documents the requester might take into account when evaluating a particular document.

"Catalog Information and Text as Indicators of Relevance" (Benenfield, Kugel, and Marcus 1978) suggests factors that may affect relevance judgments including the user's experience in the subject area, the user's prior familiarity with a document or the information provided by the document, the quality of the work, the readability of the document, the user's ability to understand the information, and the specificity of the information.

Bookstein's "Relevance" (1979) suggested that relevance be defined "as the relation between an individual, at the time he senses a need for information, and a document" (p. 269), and pointed out that relevance was not the same as topicality (p. 270). He noted that systems cannot predict the relevance of documents with certainty; only the requester can evaluate relevance (p. 269). Boyce (1982) believed "that any satisfaction of the of the user's need will be highly subjective, and dependent on the knowledge state of the requestor" (p. 105). In "Beyond Topicality," he defined relevance as a two-stage system, including topicality (aboutness) and informativeness (meaning).

MacMullin and Taylor (1984) believe information retrieval systems need to deal with matching dimensions of the user's problem situation with information traits of documents. Their article "Problem Dimensions and Information Traits" describe information traits as attributes of documents that can define ways in which information can be identified and presented, and which are characteristic of good documents as subject descriptors. They also suggested a number of problem dimensions, which are characteristics that go "beyond specific subject matter," and "establish criteria for judging the relevance of information to a problem or a class of problems" (p. 102). These problem dimensions include the design versus discovery focus of the problem; the extent to which the problem is well structured or ill structured; the extent to which the problem is simple or complex; the specific versus amorphous nature of the goals; the extent to which the initial state of the problem is understood or not understood; the extent to which assumptions within the problem are generally agreed upon or not agreed upon, and explicit or not explicit; the extent to which the solution will be presented as a familiar pattern or as a new pattern; the magnitude of risk involved in the situation; the extent to which the solution is or is not susceptible to empirical analysis; and the internal versus the external imposition of the problem onto the user (pp. 102-8).

Beghtol's "Bibliographic Classification Theory and Text Linguistics" (1986) contrasts discussing aboutness (extensional aboutness) with meaning (intensional aboutness) using van Dijk's theory of aboutness.

Research conducted for use in the improvement of information retrieval systems reveals significant empirical data about criteria used by researchers to make relevance/evaluative judgments. In "The Concept of 'Relevance' in Information Science" (1970), based on evidence from landmark studies, Saracevic summarized the major factors affecting relevance judgments as:

1. judges' subject expertise at the various stages of research;
2. judges' subject knowledge;
3. judges' academic and professional training;
4. a document's intended use; and
5. stylistic characteristics of documents. (p. 136)

In as much as items one through four are a given in research conducted by faculty members who know the major journals, are familiar with the published research in their areas and have decided for what purpose the information will be used, it is fair to say that average college-level students do not have the advantage of the aforementioned skills.

Dissertations by Schamber (*User's Criteria for Evaluation in Multimedia Information Seeking and Use Situations*, 1991), Park (*The Nature of Relevance in Information Retrieval: An Empirical Study*, 1992), and Barry (*The Identification of User Relevance Criteria and Document Characteristics: Beyond the Topical Approach to Information Retrieval*, 1993) reveal specific information about relevance judgments solicited directly from users. Empirical evidence of user-based relevance research was the subject of the previously mentioned 1994 issue of *JASIS*, and has also appeared in the information science literature by Schamber and Bateman (1996), Cool et al. (1993), and Nilan, Peek, and Snyder (1988).

Schamber's 1991 dissertation examined criteria used by professional users of weather information (n=30). Her analysis revealed ten broad-level criteria, and twenty-two subcategories of criteria (pp. 115-24).

Park's 1992 dissertation "was concerned with users' evaluative attitudes and behaviors in accepting or rejecting citations from a document retrieval system." This research provided a "theoretical" framework for the organization of user-centered criteria used in relevance judgments. In a 1993 article, "The Nature of Relevance in Information Retrieval," she reported on a number of criteria which contributed to users' selection of a citation which fall within a framework: the interpretation of a citation, internal context or experience, external context or search, and problem context or content (p. 329).

Nilan, Peek, and Snyder (1988) explored users' criteria for source evaluation, focusing on users in serious life- and health-related situations in "A Methodology for Tapping User Evaluation Behaviors." Most of the sources were human or interpersonal: self (experience, knowledge, logic); relationship to me (user); relationship to others; love; power or control; logical deduction; social pressure; uncertainty; serendipity; appearance; confidentiality; agreement or confirmation; financial considerations; only feasible source or method; best source or method; ease of access; ease of use; and source has access to technology or equipment.

In her discussion of these user-based studies, Barry (1993) noted that these studies yielded a number of implications:

1.   The theories that factors other than topicality, that were suggested as influencing users' evaluations of information is supported;
2.   There is a great deal of overlap between the criteria from empirical studies and the criteria previously suggested in the literature; and
3.   Users are apparently able to recognize non-topical aspects of information that are influencing their evaluations. (p. 151)

Barry's 1993 dissertation (n=18), which attempted to explore the relevance judgment process as it applied to textual information provided by documents, revealed twenty-three categories of relevance criteria in seven categories. Four categories of traits were identified: (1) document trait (characteristics that pertained to the physical format or actual publication of the document), (2) source traits (document characteristics that pertained to the intellectual source of the document), (3) reference traits (the provision of additional sources of information by the document), and (4) information content (all aspects of information content were coded information content as a result of the difficulty in obtaining high levels of intercoder reliability measures) (p. 76-79).

Su's 1991 dissertation, *An Investigation to Find Appropriate Measures for Evaluating Interactive Information Retrieval*, and a subsequent 1993 publication, "Is Relevance an Adequate Criterion for Retrieval System Evaluation," analyzed explanations from users about their ratings of overall success of searches and found twenty-six success dimensions (criteria). In comparing these criteria with the twenty information retrieval performance measures, she found that seventeen were new or had no counterparts. System capabilities was the most frequently mentioned dimension.

In "Characteristics of Texts Affecting Relevance Judgments" (1993), Cool et al. identified at least sixty criteria upon which users based their judgments of document usefulness. These criteria were grouped into six categories:

1. Topic (How a document relates to a person's interest);
2. Content/information (Characterization of what is "in" the document itself);
3. Format (Formal characteristics of the document);
4. Presentation (How a document is written/presented);
5. Values (Dimensions of judgment—these are modifiers of other facets); and
6. Oneself (Relationship between person's situation and the other facets). (p. 79)

Thomas's 1993 pilot study investigated criteria (situational factors) that contribute to new doctoral student's assessments of information as they interact in an unfamiliar environment. In "Information-Seeking and the Nature of Relevance: Ph.D. Student Orientation as an Exercise in Information Retrieval," she identified eighteen criteria in four categories: information and knowledge sources; feelings of uncertainty; endurance and coordination (responding to demands of the program); and establishing professional relationships. She also identified and described uncertainty factors as affective (needing, self-confirmation and status); pragmatic and cultural (understanding procedures and expectations); and academic (understanding requirements) (p. 27).

In 1994, Howard conducted a study to identify users' personal constructs or abstract structures underlying their concept of relevance or pertinence. In "Pertinence as Reflected in Personal Constructs" she found that most of the constructs fell into two categories: topicality (subject matter and document characteristics); and informativeness (related to the user's problem situation).

Specific Theory

Schamber, Eisenberg, and Nilan (1990) as well as Park (1994) have called for a theory of user-based relevance. Schamber et al., after a critical review of the research by Cuadra and Katter (1967a) and Rees and Schultz (1967), concluded that "researchers must focus on the perceptions of end-users in real information need situations" (p. 763). Park agreed and offered that "Relevance from a user's view cannot be isolated from an individual's particular situation . . . our efforts need to be focused on discovering the meaning experienced by a user within this context" (pp. 136-37).

Ellis, in "Theory and Explanation in Information Retrieval Research" (1984), and Meadow's "Relevance?" (1985), and "Problems of Information Science Research—An Opinion Paper" (1986), questioned the validity and reliability of the use of relevance as a criteria of measurement. This was later confirmed by Park (1994). Similar criticism on the use of relevance as a criteria of measurement has been found in work by Saracevic (1970), Swanson (1977), Bar-Hillel (1960), and Fairthorne (1963). Nevertheless, the concept has continued to be discussed in the literature and in relation to the effectiveness of information retrieval systems; and Froehlich (1994), in his introduction to the *JASIS* special topics issue on relevance research, reported that the diverse theoretical methods used in that issue by Sutton (mental models), Howard (personal construct), Hersh (iterative), Park, and Barry (naturalistic), Janes, and Su, who questioned the traditional system approaches, "indicate that relevance judgments can be evaluated and measured, but only in the context of specific information systems employed by uses for similar tasks" (pp. 126-27).

Discussions of the many definitions of relevance can be found in Rees and Schultz (1967), Saracevic (1970), and Regazzi's "Performance Measures for Information Retrieval Systems" (1988); as well as in Saracevic's 1975 seminal paper on relevance, "Relevance: A Review of and a Framework for the Thinking on Notion in Information Science," in which he discussed and synthesized many of the definitions represented in the literature. The often quoted 1990 article by Schamber et al. reviewed more than three decades of professional and research literature in their quest for the meaning of relevance and to determine the role that relevance plays in information behavior. They pointed out that there was clearly a confusion of terminology in the literature, and offered an excellent argument for a dynamic, user-oriented definition of relevance. Froehlich (1994) argued that "'Relevance' as used in relevance judgments by end-users cannot and never will be defined in a clear and precise sense" (p. 128). He believed that the Cartesian model of definitions is not the answer when considering a definition of relevance and noted, "If information scientists have not achieved a consensus at this point in time, it seems unlikely they ever will." He concludes that "Information scientists have to be faithful to the phenomena they are investigating, by employing appropriate methodologies" (p. 128).

Volumes 1 and 2 of *Factors Determining the Performance of Indexing Systems* (1966) by Cleverdon and Keen are commonly referred to as the The Cranfield Tests. These have served as the primary model for information retrieval research for more than a quarter of a century. This model involves selecting several recently published research papers, asking the author to provide, in the form of a question, the basic problem of the article, and also any problems encountered during the writing of the article (p. 16). This methodology was examined by Harter (1971), Swanson (1971), and later Park (1994), and all confirmed that there were design flaws in this method, particularly relating to the expert relevance judgments process.

In these tests and subsequent research using similar methodologies, relevance is defined as "reflecting aboutness," "on the topic," or "on the subject." Many authors have written and conducted studies using this definition including Eisenberg and Schamber (1988). Criticism of the lack of a more user-centered focus is evident in the literature (see W. S. Cooper 1973; Foskett 1974; Kemp 1974; Swanson 1986; Wilson 1973). Park later summarized the literature and noted that all "Introduced the notion of user-based relevance [when] making the distinction between relevance and pertinence" (p. 135).

User-oriented definitions vary widely in the literature and Schamber et al. (1990) noted that taken together, "These definitions describe relevance broadly in terms of conceptual relatedness, usefulness, pertinence, or satisfaction" (p. 759). Other authors who have included these concepts in their relevance discussions include Cuadra and Katter (1967a), Paisley (1968), Rees and Schultz (1967), and Saracevic (1970, 1975).

Relevance is also viewed by many as a multidimensional concept. Cuadra and Katter (1967a) conducted experimental research on relevance judgments and identified fourteen categories of use orientations (criteria); and, Rees and Schultz's 1967 results from "A Field Experimental Approach to the Study of Relevance Assessments in Relation to Document Searching" showed that "individual differences did appear to affect relevance judgements, especially where the judges and document/document representation varied" (p. 763).

Schamber et al. (1990) identified four characteristics common to the research conducted by Cuadra and Katter (1967a), and Rees and Schultz (1967)which make them essential to understanding relevance:

1.   Each study acknowledged the centrality of the user to the relevance judgment process;
2.   Each study named about 40 possible variables, and produced findings about the effects of some variables that have become widely accepted;
3.   Each study failed to settle on a definition of relevance; and,
4.   Each study is still unreplicated. (p. 763)

Model Framework

In order to place the concepts of relevance, evaluation, and information literacy in the proper context, it is necessary to construct a conceptual model that allows us to review the literature so that it focuses on the most critical areas. The proposed framework of the model includes the college-level students' exposure (Ex) to the information literacy skills environment, their experience (Ep) with these skills, and their relationship (R) with the faculty/advisor. This model also includes two major areas of information literacy, performance (P) and attitude (A). The performance area refers to the students' level of performance when actually answering queries that illustrate evaluation skills and abilities; and the attitude refers to the students' attitude toward all ten information literacy skills. The model also includes the level of relevance/evaluation. For the purposes of this study, it is assumed that performance and attitude are predictors of relevance/evaluation. The model can be expressed as follows:

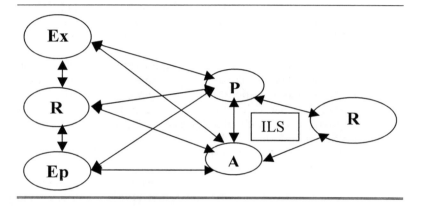

Figure 3.2. Model of the relevance relationship to information literacy skills (ILS).

After developing the model (figure 3.2) based on a review of the literature, it was decided that the best way to present the professional and research literature in the Review of the Literature section, was to interpret it through the model presented above. Much of this literature deals with the pertinent factors of the model as a broad concept.

This review is not meant to be a comprehensive review of the information literacy or relevance/evaluation literature. It will only cover research which best represents the elements of the model as shown above. Much of the research includes relevant findings for more than one element.

Predicting Performance and Attitude

This section will discuss the elements of the model which represent a relationship with the performance and attitudinal aspects of the information literacy skills subset. For the purposes of this study, and derived from the model (figure 3.2) developed from the literature review, it is assumed that the elements of exposure, relationship with faculty/advisor, and experience are correlated and are predictors of the performance and attitude components of information literacy skills.

The role of exposure represents the level of exposure users have to the information literacy skills environment (e.g., library orientation, library tour); and the role of experience represents the level of experience users have in using the information literacy skills (e.g., knowledge of bibliographic style, publication cycles of published literature, database selection, scope of topic). The relationship between the student and the faculty/advisor, in the classroom or as a dissertation/thesis advisor, is included in this section as a predictor of performance and attitude. It is presumed that this factor is an integral part of the information literacy process.

The relevant research and professional literature presented here will be discussed in the context of the instrument elements. Thus, each section will be guided by relevant findings from Morner (1993), whose study serves as the foundation for the current study.

Role of Exposure

Graduate Students

In her 1993 dissertation, *A Test of Library Research Skills for Education Doctoral Students*, Morner conducted preliminary research in order to learn more about how graduate students use the library. She interviewed ten doctoral education students and asked questions about their exposure to the library research environment, possible library frustration, familiarity with library staff specializing in education, and other questions about their research behavior. An analysis of these interviews provided Morner with the basic data for her survey instrument. Answers to queries were categorized based on a review of the literature. The following items from Morner's list of problems derived from the data fall into the exposure category of the current study (categorized by Morner as attitude, access, information-seeking behavior, and personal factors) and include:

1. Library anxiety, based either on previous bad experience in library or poor library skills, is prevalent among graduate students.
2. Some graduate students are not library users, because they have not needed to use the library for previous academic work. Many may rely on departmental, personal, or faculty collections for information for course papers.
3. Graduate students are frequently unwilling to ask for help. They may think their question is stupid, or that others expect that, at the doctoral level, they already know how to use research libraries. Some may not want to bother librarians, or think that asking librarians for help is "cheating."
4. International graduate students may have more difficulty working in American academic libraries. In addition to language and cultural barriers, international graduate students are not accustomed to public services staff, [such as] reference librarians, and open stacks. Libraries in many other countries are less accessible to students than those in the USA.
5. Graduate students lack time to gain a thorough understanding of library research. Students may not realize how time-consuming library research can be, or they may be busy with course work, jobs, or personal responsibilities, which compete for their time and attention. (pp. 147-52)

The preceding problem areas are supported in research by Toomer (1993) and Park (1986a), who found that students beginning graduate schools are not sufficiently informed about libraries. In "Information Needs: Implications for the Academic Library," Park found that 80 percent of those surveyed (n=100) mentioned time restraints as a perceived barrier. Difficulties in locating sources and in understanding library procedures were also perceived as barriers by 51 percent and 44 percent of those surveyed respectively (p. 14). Another Park survey, "Information Seeking Behavior: An Introductory Examination (1986b), (n=25) yielded similar results (pp. 19, 28).

Questions 9 through 12 on the "Morner Test of Library Research Skills," duplicated below, were designed to illustrate the student's exposure to the library research environment. They required an answer of "yes" or "no."

9.   Tour or physical orientation to the library.
10. Library instruction in class.
11. Lecture or workshop in library.
12. Intensive one-on-one instruction with librarian. (p. 64)

Of the 149 doctoral education students tested by Morner, nearly 39 percent reported that they had no library instruction; almost 17 percent reported a minimal level of instruction (defined by Morner as individuals who answered yes to tour and no to the other forms of instruction); almost 35 percent reported a moderate level of instruction (defined as individuals who answered yes to tour and yes to one or more of the other forms of instruction); and less than 3 percent reported a high level of instruction (defined as individuals who answered yes to all four instruction questions) (p. 86). Her final test analysis revealed the following:

1. There was no difference between the scores of full-time and part-time students;
2. Students with more computer experience had slightly greater scores than those with less computer experience;
3. Students who reported more library exposure tended to have progressively higher scores than students who reported a minimal level of instruction; and,
4. Students who reported no instruction performed slightly better than those who had taken a tour. (p. 115)

Morner offered that the reason for this discrepancy could be that "students who come to their doctoral programs with greater knowledge and experience with library research . . . may have not felt the need for further instruction" (p. 115).

Morner's results confirm that the level of exposure to a library research skills environment has an impact on the performance and attitudes of users. General findings from Morner are supported by research from Libutti (1991, p. 12), Farid, Snyder, Palmquist, and Dull (1984, pp. 96-97), and Thaxton (1985, p. 123). Findings and conclusions on research on adult learners and bibliographic instruction by Toomer (1993) are compatible with Morner's. In Toomer's dissertation, *Adult Learner Perceptions of Bibliographic Instructional Services,* (n=25), he concluded, among other things, that:

1. A review of research and published literature suggests that college and university libraries have not responded adequately to the learning support needs of the increasingly large adult student populations on their campuses;
2. Most bibliographic instruction programs are designed around group processes—orientation sessions, lectures, and personal guidance—as opposed to the affirmed preference, represented in the literature by research, for programs that allow for self-learning. Even current printed materials have continued to focus on providing directions to locations of information and not on how to use the information in a variety of learning situations;

3. Self-learning methodologies for instructional delivery have not
    yet been utilized effectively, especially computer and other elec-
    tronic multi-media;
4. Perceptions of adult learners in the colleges and universities
    studied suggest librarians may not always be fully utilized by
    adult students as a learning resource; and although adult students
    are fully aware of the available bibliographic instructional ser-
    vices and programs of the library, they still perceive the need of
    additional bibliographic instructional activities. (pp. 81-82)

Toomer's findings on self-learning methodologies support similar findings by Libutti (1991, p. 13).

Alire's 1984 dissertation, *A Nationwide Survey of Education Doctoral Students' Attitudes,* included a self-report section on their exposure to libraries. Of the 898 students surveyed, 45 percent reported they
would support a required course in library instruction at the graduate
level, and almost half reported they would take library instruction as an
elective. Fifty-seven percent of those reported that they thought they
needed bibliographic instruction, and 48 percent reported they learned
to use the library in high school. Seventy-seven percent reported that
they thought knowledge of the library and its resources was important
to success in their programs, and 63 percent felt that library usage was
a factor of success (p. 72).

Parrish (1989a) conducted a large scale study of the research behavior of graduate students at Bowling Green University. An analysis
of the data collected revealed 22 percent of those surveyed reported that
they attended the university-wide, week-long orientation sessions, and
an even smaller percentage selected library/research skills instruction
(p. 645). Interviews, about the skills necessary to succeed in the field
and how those skills are learned, were conducted with departmental
chairs and graduate advisers. Parrish reported that the faculty "assumed
that students know how to do research by the time they get to graduate
school." However, she found that the students surveyed "experienced
difficulty with each step of the research process" (p. 646). An additional Parrish study (1989b) reported the following in terms of exposure:

- 38 percent had a library tour;
- 34 percent had a library seminar during orientation; and
- 26 percent had a presentation by a librarian in class. (p. 61)

Other methods which were useful in reducing the amount of time students spent looking for materials included: 55 percent requested assistance at the reference desk; and 39 percent used guidebooks. Ten per-

cent of those surveyed reported they had received little or no library instruction before the research the study chronicled; 82 percent reported they had library experience via undergraduate courses; 36 percent through independent studies; 28 percent during master's coursework, and 13 percent during master's theses. Thirty-two percent of those surveyed said they had consulted previously with a librarian about research; however, 35 percent were not aware of the availability of such a service (p. 61). Parrish (1989a) concluded that regardless of the faculty's views, graduate students reported that faculty members were a key factor in their graduate education, and also described them as helpful (p. 646).

In 1995, Simon's "Information Retrieval Techniques" examined the strategies (successful and unsuccessful) used by 112 graduate students to complete literature searches. She believed that by studying these sessions, librarian educators could determine the types of training this population needed. The demographic section of her questionnaire included a section on exposure (categorized by Simon as knowledge of search methods). Simon found that of all 112 participants, only thirty (26.78 percent) reported they had prior formal or informal instruction (e.g., tour, seminar, handbook, or course) before participating in the study (pp. 53-54, 59). More than half the population surveyed (59.6 percent) taught themselves to use the library. Tied at second place, reported by 20.7 percent of the population, was learning from a friend, written material, class, or other and requesting help from library staff.

In 1984, in the third edition of *The Adult Learner: A Neglected Species*, Knowles noted the assumptions about adult learners as follows:

1. Adults learn best when they have a strong need to learn something;
2. As adults, learners are self-directed, independent and will seek out what they need to learn; and
3. Individualized learning works best for adults because adult learners come to school with varied backgrounds and experiences. (p. 164)

Knowles (1990) added a fourth important characteristic of how adults learn—

4. Adults are task-oriented in their learning; learning best when learned in the context of use. (p. 164)

Morner (1993) listed characteristics of adult learners, decidedly different from those of a child, as:

1. Multiple demands and responsibilities in terms of time, energy, emotions, and roles;
2. Greater self-determination and acceptance of responsibility; and
3. Greater need to cope with transitions and with existential issues of competence, emotions, autonomy, identity, relationships, purpose, and integrity. (p. 10)

These assumptions about adult learners are significant in view of the ways in which exposure to these environments has traditionally been conducted. In developing library and instructional programs for this population (adult learners), it is necessary to understand how and why they learn in order for programmatic efforts to be successful. The professional and research literature on adult learners and how they learn differently from the K-12 population is important in this regard.

Undergraduate Students

Sheridan's (1986) article, "Andragogy: A New Concept for Academic Libraries" focused on adult learner undergraduates. She pointed out "that the adult student has a preferred style of learning." The andragogical model is often difficult to impose as a result of the "traditional learning styles of most adult students and the traditional teaching styles to which they were exposed in elementary and high school" (p. 162).

The findings of a 1988 article, "Information Seeking Behavior," by Osiobe on Nigerian undergraduates resulted in greater efforts to include use of the library in the mandatory general studies course at Nigerian universities. This is a for credit course which the students take seriously; and Osiobe pointed out that the library orientation program is not taken seriously by students (p. 346). Osiobe reported that "The inclusion of the use of library resources as part of the GS [General Studies] course gives students the opportunity to learn about the use of various bibliographic instruction tools in their specific disciplines and how to conduct a literature search in the library" (p. 346).

Damko's 1990 master's research paper, *Student Attitudes Toward Bibliographic Instruction*, was a study to determine what value, if any, college students placed on library use instruction. She surveyed students from a variety of colleges and universities to determine whether a library use course or program was offered at their schools, and if they thought it would be a worthwhile venture (p. 15). Damko's survey instrument included two demographic questions and thirteen designed to measure the current and general library use practices, the availability of library use instruction, and attitudes. She reported that overall, students felt that library instruction was a good idea, but "apparently for students other than themselves." Nearly 59 percent of the students taught themselves to use the library. Unfortunately the study does not reveal how well these students taught themselves. Damko reported that "a student who knows how to use the card catalog considers him/herself a library expert" (p. 27). She concluded that these experts were simply not aware of their previously inadequate skills with the automation of many resources.

Although Damko found that self-teaching was the second most popular way of acquiring library skills, the number one method was high school instruction (72.39 percent). Damko wondered how much of this instruction was actually remembered, how much was irrelevant and how important technology was currently in library research. She also found that 46.06 percent learned to use the library as a part of freshman orientation, and 13.50 percent learned from a course (80.37 percent reported not having taken a course).

Of those who had taken a course, 16.77 percent found the course helpful. Twenty-five percent of those surveyed said they thought a course in library instruction would be helpful, and nearly 73 percent said they would benefit from a library use course. Of those surveyed, 40.24 percent said they would take a course because they believed it would be easy and they could improve their grade point average; 59.15 percent would take a course because it would help them to write better papers; and 72.12 percent would take a course because it would help them to locate materials. Nearly 73 percent said they thought a course would be helpful (p. 26).

Kester's 1994 study can be considered companion to Damko's in that she sought to find out if secondary school library and information skills were actually transferred from high school to college. In "Secondary School Library and Information Skills. Are they Transferred from High School to College?," Kester's statistical analysis (n=300) revealed only a few college students (freshmen) were influenced by college library instruction; there was little integration of library skills with course content; little evidence of team-teaching between teachers and librarians; and the students (31.7 percent) seemed to only be familiar with *Reader's Guide*, in spite of the availability of CD-ROM reference tools at 85 percent of the schools in the area. She also found that most of the students were unable to identify an on-line catalog or Boolean searching.

Kester concluded that "High school library skills instruction appears to have little carry over or effect on students going on to college, with but a few exceptions." She continued and hypothesized whether the "little integration of library skills and course content" and "team teaching between the librarian and the classroom teacher explain[ed] the small carry over of library skills" (p. 17).

Herring's 1994 dissertation recommended that additional research should be done "on the problem solving skills that are introduced in high school to determine if indeed any transfer of learning is carrying over into the college environment" (p. 17).

Citing Goodin's 1991 research article, "The Transferability of Library Research Skills from High Schools to College," Herring (1994) noted that it supported the concept that information skills should be taught in the order of basic skills (p. 14). Goodin's research (n=159) investigated, among other things, the transferability of library research skills from high school to college. She stated that "If . . . it is essential that students should have acquired certain basic skills necessary to conduct undergraduate research, it becomes obvious that such skills should be taught while these students are still in high school" (p. 33). Goodin concluded that based on her study, the most transferable skill acquired by the students studied was learning to use the librarian as a resource (p. 35). She also concluded that an instruction program for high school students has a significant impact on the attitudes and performance, but, based on her results, the transfer of these beneficial effects was less clear. In enumerating study implications for practitioners, Goodin noted:

1. College students exposed to the program of instruction indicated through narrative responses that they were able to utilize effectively the research skills learned in high school when conducting college-level research.
2. College students indicated that the high school program of instruction should be made available to all college-bound seniors.
3. The findings of this study strongly indicate the importance of the school library media specialist assuming the role of educator. To facilitate the transfer of library research skills from one grade level to another, school library media specialists at all grade levels need to consider themselves full participants in the total educational program of their respective institutions. (pp. 36-37)

In one of the few information literacy studies, Maughan (1994) surveyed graduating seniors in the political science and sociology departments at the University of California at Berkeley (U. C. Berkeley). Maughan found that of the 71 percent responding political science seniors, and 56 percent graduating sociology majors (n=255), seven of the eight high scorers in sociology had library instruction, and 62 percent of the high scoring political science graduates had taken library instruction while attending U. C. Berkeley.

Geffert and Bruce (1997) conducted a longitudinal study of the effectiveness of bibliographic instruction over the entire undergraduate experience. In their article, "Whither BI? Assessing Perceptions of Research Skills over an Undergraduate Career," they requested information on exposure and found that 27 percent of the 216 students surveyed from 22 disciplines reported they had attended 1 bibliographic instruction session; 31 percent had attended 2 sessions; 20 percent had attended 3 sessions; and 16 percent had attended 4 sessions. Six percent reported they had not any attended sessions on bibliographic instruction (p. 411).

Role of Experience

Graduate Students

In "The Role of Instruction in the Academic Library" (1973) Watkins was among the first to document graduate student's lack of library skills. Watkins noted, "Many a graduate student goes through his course work and the preparation of a dissertation woefully lacking in bibliographical knowledge and unaware of important reference works in his field" (p. 9). Research by Hernandez (1985) found that graduate students have the most difficulty with the literature review and did not have enough experience or knowledge of libraries to use them effectively.

Morner's (1993) preliminary research found that "Students may not understand organization of [the] library. They may be unfamiliar with [the] Library of Congress system, or they may not know basic categories/formats of information in libraries, such as reference books, periodicals, indexes, microfilm, or government documents" (p. 148).

Morner reported that although almost 50 percent of the 149 doctoral education students surveyed knew the Library of Congress classification section for education books, only 38 percent knew and could identify the Superintendent of Documents classification number used to classify government documents in depository collections and in academic institutions. This is significant because the U.S. government is a major publisher of materials in North America, and the U.S. Department of Education publishes and distributes a great deal of education-related material.

Morner also found that a little more than half of those surveyed knew where to find *ERIC*[1] documents, a major information resource in education, and only 56 percent knew the best way to locate dissertations from other institutions.

"A Study of Information Seeking Behavior of Ph.D. Students in Selected Disciplines" (1984), by Farid, Snyder, Palmquist, and Dull, based on Farid's 1982 dissertation, surveyed sixty-nine Ph.D. students from a variety of disciplines at Syracuse University. The researchers found that the students ranked the importance of the library based on the library's collections in their discipline. They also found that of all the resources listed, print and non-print, the card catalog and the on-line catalog were the most frequently used resource, selected by a total of 89.1 percent of those surveyed; however, only 53 percent of the students completing coursework frequently used abstracts and indexes. Nearly 30 percent of those at the dissertation stage reported frequently using abstracts and indexes, and surprisingly 18.9 percent reported not using abstracts and indexes at all (pp. 88-89). Less than 7 percent of those taking coursework, and 13.5 percent of those at the dissertation stage reported frequent use of interlibrary loan (ILL); and 24.3 percent of those at the dissertation stage reported not using ILL services at all. Almost 33 percent of those at the dissertation stage reported using reference frequently, 43.2 percent reported occasional use, and 21.6 percent reported not making use of reference at all. Sixteen point two percent at the dissertation stage reported frequent use of online searching, 13.5 percent occasional use, and 43.2 percent reported not using online searching at all (pp. 92-93).

In 1985, Thaxton reported in "Dissemination and Use of Information by Psychology Faculty and Graduate Students," that of the fifty-seven surveyed, 79 percent reported that they used *Psychological Abstracts* most frequently (defined as used at least twice a quarter). Another important source, *Social Science Citation Index*, which Thaxton reports was advertised heavily by librarians and of critical importance to the faculty, was used frequently by only 19 percent of the students. Forty-four percent reported they used it sometimes and 37 percent reported no use at all (p. 122). When broken down to students who had bibliographic instruction as compared to those who did not, the following results were revealed:

- 33 percent reporting instruction used *Social Science Citation Index* frequently; 40 percent used it sometimes; and 27 percent reported never using it;
- 14 percent reporting no instruction used *Social Science Citation Index* frequently; 50 percent used it sometimes; and 36 percent reported never using it;
- 93 percent reporting instruction used *Psychological Abstracts* frequently; and 7 percent used it sometimes;
- 76 percent reporting no instruction used *Psychological Abstracts* frequently; and 24 percent reported never using it;

- 33 percent reporting instruction used *Dissertation Abstracts* frequently; 47 percent used it sometimes; and 20 percent reported never using it;
- 17 percent reporting no instruction used *Dissertation Abstracts* frequently; 55 percent used it sometimes; and 28 percent reported never using it; and
- 60 percent reporting instruction used *Online Computer Literature Searching*; and 38 percent reporting no instruction had used it. (p. 123)

Compton (1989) surveyed doctoral students in science education (n=30) using a survey instrument divided into three parts: data on the use of library resources during the coursework phase of the doctoral program; data on the use of library resources during the dissertation phase of the doctoral program; and for students who had completed the program, the library resources they did not use while in graduate school. Compton found that while completing course assignments many students relied extensively or frequently on manual searches of journals (80 percent); manual literature searches (70 percent); and citations from other sources (73 percent) for information identification. The subject card catalog was used extensively or frequently by only 20 percent of the sample, the on-line catalog was used by only 40 percent; and computerized literature searches were used even less frequently with only 37 percent using them extensively or frequently (pp. 24-25). Usage during the dissertation phase was more prevalent with extensive or frequent use of manual literature searches reported by 81 percent; manual searches of journals by 89 percent; and citations from other sources for information identification by 77 percent of the sample. Forty-two percent reported rare or no use of the on-line catalog during this time (pp. 26-27).

Libutti (1991) surveyed master's and doctoral level education students and as a part of her survey, included a list of education-related resources. She found that only 50 percent of the doctoral students surveyed noted two prominent education titles, *Psychological Abstracts* and *Current Index to Journals in Education*. Other important sources were not used by the majority of those surveyed.

Morner's analysis of test items relevant to experience (coded as intellectual access, content sources, bibliographic sources, and developing topic) revealed that:

1. Graduate students may have difficulty locating materials in the stacks because of incomplete call numbers, and incorrect call numbers, or not understanding decimals. (p. 148)
2. Information overload is a problem for all library users: finding too much information and not knowing how to deal with it.

> Graduate students may use information overload coping tech-
> niques that may not yield the best results. These include select-
> ing the first few articles on a topic rather than evaluating a bibli-
> ography, or browsing stacks or journals rather than using
> indexes or catalogs. (p. 151)

Morner found that although 65 percent of those surveyed understood how computerized databases work on a search, and 71 percent
understood Boolean logic, and knew how to limit a search yielding a
large number of citations; less than 50 percent knew the purpose of
truncation, only 40 percent understood the advantage of keyword
searching in an on-line catalog, and only 30 percent understood the
relationship between the Library of Congress classification scheme of
books on the shelf, and using the Library of Congress subject headings
to search the on-line catalog (pp. 95-96). Morner's additional analysis
of experience items found that:

3. When students find information in [sic] library by accident, they
    become anxious about their lack of library research skills.
4. Library knowledge of graduate students varies among graduate
    students. Some know a great deal, others have not used research
    libraries before. Graduate students frequently teach each other
    and pass on bits of information gleaned from experience. (p.
    151)

Morner reported that more than 90 percent of those surveyed understood the most important first step in library research as knowing the
research problem; however, only 29 percent understood what to do with
a given topic before beginning a search. Less than 50 percent of the
students understood which search strategy, of those given, was least
likely to aid in narrowing a broad topic; and only 44 percent selected,
when given a particular topic, the option which represented the first
step in collecting information. Conversely, more than 65 percent understood when they were nearing the completion of a literature search (pp.
95-96).

Morner noted that "Some students at the graduate level are still
using skills gained in high school or during the first years of college to
attempt doctoral level research" (p. 22). An analysis of her findings on
items in content sources and bibliographic sources categories reveals
the following:

- 8 percent knew the best way to identify recent research that follows up a previously written key article;
- 37 percent did not know the advantage of using a printed source
  over its electronic counterpart;

- 54 percent knew the scope of *ERIC*, a critical education source;
- 41 percent knew the difference between a subject encyclopedia, a subject dictionary, a subject database, and a subject related abstracting source; and
- 11 percent knew where to find subject related statistical data. (pp. 95-96)

Undergraduate Students

Reed's 1974 research (n=39), "Information-Seeking Behavior of College Students Using a Library to do Research," was conducted to "assess the bibliographic search process of students." He concluded:

1. In general, students seem poorly skilled in use of a college library;
2. Students seem not to have received sufficient instruction to significantly improve their use of a library over those students who have not received instruction to use a library;
3. Students [studied] using the card catalog, tend to search most frequently by subject;
4. Students seem to be unskilled in translating their questions into terms compatible with the library system;
5. Students frequently fail to consult appropriate, key bibliographic and information sources;
6. Logical progression and systematic approaches to checking sources of information often appear to be absent. Subjects frequently skipped from source to source, wandered aimlessly, or made no progress, in the process of the search; and
7. The conception of research on the part of many Subjects appeared to be limited and unsophisticated—often involving little more than finding a book and checking it out of the library. (pp. 21-22)

In 1988, York, Sabol, Gratch, and Pursel interviewed 117 users of 4 computerized reference sources (on-line catalog, OCLC, *InfoTrac*, and *News Bank Electronic Index*) and found that 92 percent had used computers before. Unfortunately, a number of those surveyed were unable to accurately describe the purpose of particular computerized tools, including the on-line catalog.

Osiobe's (1988) study on the information seeking behavior of undergraduates in Nigeria found that 23.9 percent of the 502 students surveyed selected browsing as their primary source of reference to the literature. Faculty and staff and the card catalog tied at second place (17.53 percent), followed by librarians (13.15 percent), references in articles and books (12.35 percent), abstracts and indexes (7.97 percent), and colleagues (7.57 percent) (p. 340).

Ochs, Coons, Van Ostrand, and Barnes (1991) surveyed graduates of Cornell University's Mann Library's instruction program (n=317) from the business and finance school, to determine which skills were retained by students and were useful in their careers after graduation. Recent graduates were asked to evaluate the level of skill expected of them in their new positions in finding information in computerized databases and using computer telecommunications networks and software. The researchers reported that

- 52.7 percent reported they were expected to have skills in finding information in computerized databases at or above the basic level; and
- 24.2 percent were expected to have skills in computer telecommunications at or above the basic level. (p. 13)

Students were also asked to identify methods which provided an opportunity for learning skills by choosing from the following: On my own; at Cornell through academic classes; at Cornell through the Mann Library's instruction program; on the job; high school; and other. They reported that their secondary education (high school) was not an important source for learning computer skills for most students; and the library's instruction program was selected by 86 of the 317 surveyed for learning skills expected by the employer in finding information in computerized databases. Examples of these skills included finding appropriate computerized information sources; understanding how databases are organized in order to find information more effectively; searching full-text databases such as complete journal articles or other textual documents; searching numeric databases such as census data or commodity prices; and searching bibliographic databases to find references to articles, books, or reports (p. 19).

Role of Relationship with Faculty

The student's relationship with the faculty as described in the literature, is a dual one. Faculty advise students individually, and also influence students in the classroom environment. The literature reveals that the role of the faculty as advisor for undergraduates is more developmental and less likely to focus on the specifics of information literacy skills. Graduate students rely heavily on advisors, especially when completing dissertations, theses, teaching practicums, and/or research projects, and there is evidence that this relationship may be a predictor of performance and attitude.

Graduate Students

In 1976, Katz and Hartnett reported on a study of more than 700 graduate students from 5 different disciplines. In a chapter on graduate student relations with the faculty the authors noted that "the nature of the graduate student's relations with the faculty—is probably the single most salient feature of the graduate department climate" (p. 59). The authors continued and pointed out that there were two components of this relationship: accessibility and the way faculty tend to treat students (p. 64).

> Students objected most often to two sorts of things: the expectation by the faculty that they should be regarded and treated by graduate students with a sort of reverence, and the faculty attitudes toward graduate students that led to what many referred to as a state of prolonged adolescence. (p. 66)

In Bargar and Mayo-Chamberlain's 1983 essay on doctoral advising and adult development, "Advisor and Advisee Issues in Doctoral Education," the authors suggested various roles for advisor and doctoral student throughout the doctoral program as well as developmental factors. "Many graduate programs are not set up to deal . . . with the personal developmental changes that propel students back into graduate education" (p. 408). Citing McClure's 1981 dissertation, the authors also reported that there had been no research conducted on the developmental nature of the advisor/advisee relationship.

Winston and Polkosnik's 1984 article, "Advising Graduate and Professional School Students," pointed out the personal adjustments and often sacrifices graduate students make when returning to school, often after spending time in the work force. They also reported that in graduate school, once independent individuals find themselves dependent on their professors for evaluation and self-esteem. Decisions to delay beginning a family or marrying in favor of graduate school often leaves the student feeling lonely, isolated, and frustrated. Suggested roles the advisor should fill include that of reliable information source, departmental socializer, advocate, role model, occupational socializer, friend, and mentor (p. 291).

Zaporozhetz's 1987 dissertation provides insight into the advisor/advisee relationship from the faculty's point of view. In *The Dissertation Literature Review: How Faculty Advisors Prepare their Doctoral Candidates*, she surveyed education faculty (n=33) about their role in assisting graduate students with the literature review section of the dissertation, and found some resentment on the part of the faculty for having to spend time helping students who were having problems with this section. She also found that of all the chapters in the dissertation, the literature review was allocated the least amount of reading and advising time, and faculty members who served as readers admitted to not reading the literature review chapter. When queried these faculty members admitted to either not being familiar enough with the literature to have an opinion or finding the chapter uninteresting if they were familiar with it. Zaporozhetz's principal findings included, among other things:

1.   The advisors reported that they have preferences for the kinds of dissertations they will advise. Some will agree to advise dissertations in a broad scope of topics within education, putting the burden on the advisee to educate the advisor in the literature of the field; others will agree to advise dissertations only in limited narrow topic areas within education, generally their own field of expertise. The advisor's preference for a subject area is often coupled with a preference for the methodology of the dissertation which may also affect the literature review.

2.   Advisors prefer to work individually with their advisees to define such factors as focus, format, areas to be discussed, and the length of the dissertation review. The other committee members generally react to the decisions of the advisor and the candidate, but do not participate in making them.

3.   Advisors rated some sources more productive than others for dissertation literature reviews in education. The four sources rated most productive were: refereed journals, books, dissertations, and the *Resources in Education* portion of *ERIC*.

4.   Advisors reported that they had to deal with a wide range of specific problems during the early stages of advising a dissertation literature review. These included defining the nature and amount of related literature, the advisees' ability to locate the relevant literature, and their own possible limited knowledge of the advisees' dissertation field.

5.   Advisors reported that the writing of the dissertation literature review often caused advising problems. These included the inability of some candidates to organize and synthesize large groupings of literature, and to write an effective literature review.

6.   The advisors ranked the literature review lowest of five identified elements of a dissertation in the amount of time/energy they expended, and in the level of their expertise.

7.   The advisors reported different behaviors when they served as committee members. Half of the advisors in the study group reported that they carefully read the rest of the dissertation, but tended not to read the literature review. Others reported skim-

ming the literature review, and carefully reading other portions of the dissertation.

8. Advisors reported that their own dissertation writing experiences had a major influence on their own advising beliefs and behaviors.

9. Advisors reported that the dissertation literature reviews in the college of education should focus on what many identified as "representative literature" and should not attempt to be comprehensive.

10. Advisors reported they were uncomfortable with and distrustful of the new searching technologies—and some indicated an almost complete lack of understanding of indexing philosophies or appropriate use of computer search results. (pp. 131-33)

Zaporozhetz's research confirmed the 1981 research by Dreifuss which found that 91 percent of faculty members do expect their graduate students to be proficient in library research skills to conduct their literature reviews, and thus, they will not have to deal with this area in detail. "Overall," Zaporozhetz concluded, "they [advisors] felt doctoral candidates should go to the library to 'do the literature review,' come back with the results, and at that stage the advisor should offer suggestions and assist in writing and editing" (p. v). Research by Maio (1995), Nowakowski and Frick (1995), J. Thomas and Ensor (1982), J. Thomas (1994), and Lubans (1980) from the attitudinal literature on faculty confirm and support Zaporozhetz's findings.

Of special interest is a 1986 dissertation by Kammerer on the advisors' perceptions of their advising experiences with doctoral students during the dissertation process. Kammerer interviewed and analyzed data from major advisors (n=20) from the College of Education at The Ohio State University. His data analysis revealed three categories, including Student—Dissertation, under which advisors' perceptions of students research skills was revealed as a problem area (see figure 3.3).

Kammerer reported that advisors' felt the students' completion of required coursework ". . . did not assure the students' research competence." He also reported that some advisors felt pressured [by students] into committee meetings before they were ready (p. 103).

Category I	Advisor—Student Relationship

Category II	Student—Dissertation Relationship
	Topic/Problem
	Selection
	Conceptualization
	Commitment to and interest in
	    Student Attributes
	      Abilities
	      Writing Skills
	        Problem Areas for students/advisors
	          Inadequate research skills
	          Working with marginal students

Category III	Advisor—dissertation relationship

Figure 3.3. Kammerer's (1986) categories of relationships between the advisor, student, and dissertation during the dissertation experience.

Based on his findings, Kammerer reported a number of propositions and major implications for the practice of dissertation advising, including

1. Students who were self starters, had good writing skills, were independent and research competent were associated with the best advising experiences and better dissertations. Conversely, students with marginal capabilities, poor writing skills, too dependent upon their advisors were associated with more difficult advising and poorer dissertations; (p. 153)
2. Although advisors perceived the dissertation experience of their students to be creative, they offered few suggestions or examples of efforts they initiated or entertained to provide for more creative dissertation activity of their students;
3. Advisors reported that the demands of the advisor-student relationship as it relates to the advisor's time, interest in the topic, and the quality of the work often resulted in greater time demand on the advisor, a characteristic of those dissertation advising experiences perceived by the advisors as difficult or troublesome; and
4. The quality of the advisor and student interpersonal relationship related directly to the quality of the dissertation advising experience. (pp. 157-60)

Kammerer noted that advisors "perceived a [high] need for students to be able to write, conceptualize, and conduct their research on their own" (p. 153), and reported that "The dissertation should provide students with a beginning, initial research experience" (p. 157).

Other key research on advising Ph.D. students was conducted by Hockin in 1981. His research focused on the symbiotic relationship between the faculty advisor and the Ph.D. student advisee, its interrelational components and its implications for higher education. In *Symbiosis and Socialization: A Sociological Examination of Ph.D. Advising,* he contended that "in the process of professional socialization, no relationship is more pivotal than the relationship with the doctoral advisor." Using historical secondary data and a self-report questionnaire, Hockin found:

1. A small percentage of the faculty (5.5 percent) had advised a significant portion of Ph.D. recipients (approximately 30 percent) during a 23 year period;
2. Graduate advisees were more likely to select advisors on the basis of personal or interactive considerations;
3. Those advisees who selected on the basis of interactive considerations expressed more satisfaction than those who selected on the basis of career considerations;
4. Perceptions of exploitations tended to be lower among those who selected on the basis of interactive rather than career considerations; and,
5. Top advisors structured this advising component of their jobs as an orientation in the relationship on values rather than content. They also demonstrated greater flexibility in their advising styles. (pp. 51, 58)

Overall, this research supports a theory of sociality/partnership existing in this unique advising relationship between the faculty and Ph.D. students. Hockin found that the arrangement proved to be mutually beneficial for both parties involved.

McFarland and Caplow (1995) studied faculty attitudes toward doctoral students in arts and science disciplines. The authors conducted forty open-ended interviews and found that the majority of the faculty reported they had no regular or formal communication with their doctoral students, and many felt that the students were not assertive enough and not committed enough to complete the degree (pp. 6-7). The authors also reported on the faculty discussing their roles in the preparation of the students which revealed that faculty perspectives and expectations of students reflect internal contradictions (p. 14). They expected students to be assertive and independent without realizing the highly unequal power relationship between doctoral students and faculty. They also seemed to take little responsibility for the progress of their students (p. 8). These results were contradictory to recommendations of national policymakers for improving doctoral completion (p. 16).

In 1995 Lussier found that the success of doctoral students (n=102) at the University of Manitoba is affected by various components of the advisory relationship. Similar results have been reported in research by Rudd ("A New Look at Postgraduate Failure," 1985), and Girves and Wemmerus (1988) who suggested further study of the relationship between faculty and students as a function of academic discipline in "Developing Models of Graduate Student Degree Progress."

Research by Manis, Frazier-Kouassi, Hollenshead, and Burkam (1993) at the Center for the Education of Women, University of Michigan, on graduate students (n=1008) found that mentoring and advising are key factors in the graduate experience and noted similar studies with similar findings conducted at Princeton, Carnegie Mellon, and Berkeley. In *A Survey of the Graduate Experience: Sources of Satisfaction and Dissatisfaction among Graduate Students at the University of Michigan*, the researchers reported that "the quality of the academic programs and faculty was cited most frequently as a source of satisfaction with their academic experiences in open-ended responses" (p. iii).

Overall, libraries (library facilities) ranked in the highest level of satisfaction with nearly 75 percent being moderately or very satisfied (p. iii). Satisfaction with academic and career advising were less prevalent with the following percentages reported for each category: moderate or very satisfied: 33 percent for academic advising and 25 percent for career advising; moderate or very dissatisfied: 27 percent for academic advising and 38 percent for career advising. Nearly half of the sample reported moderate to high satisfaction for guidance in research activities; and overall, 33 percent of the women and 24 percent of the men were very moderately or moderately dissatisfied with the extent of mentoring (p. 3). Researchers also reported on queries related to the students satisfaction about specific advisor qualities. Ninety-six percent of Ph.D. students (n=686) and 88 percent of master's students (n=322) reported having a faculty advisor. At both levels, women were likely to report their advisor had been appointed by the department (Ph.D.—45 percent; master's—32 percent). Other relevant findings include:

- 75 percent moderately or very satisfied with advisors' substantive knowledge in relevant disciplines;
- 50 percent moderately or very satisfied with their advisors' knowledge of university, school, or departmental policies and procedures;
- More than 50 percent were moderately or very satisfied with their advisors' qualities of empathy, kindness, understanding, or ability to be a good listener; and,

- 42 percent moderately or very satisfied with their advisors' efforts to provide specific suggestions or guidance about courses to take, or advice about desirable research experience or jobs. (p 4)

Some open-ended comments related to the extent and quality of mentoring received by students are relevant to this study.

Faculty are so busy with research, recruiting other faculty, and general administration that they often have little time to spare with students. Students need to be really pushy to get attention.

I have received no mentoring at U-M. Faculty are too busy with their other jobs or doing research to care about being a mentor. (p. 5)

Overall, lack of mentorship or guidance was one of the most selected areas for factors that might have significantly slowed progress or caused particular difficulties (p. 6). Twenty-one percent of those responding reported inadequate or misguided advising or mentoring when asked the question: "What aspects of your experiences at U-M have been most disturbing, disappointing, or problematic?" (p. 6).

In *Graduates and ABDs in Colleges of Education: Characteristics and Implications for the Structures of Doctoral Programs* (1995), a compilation of symposium papers on degree completion and noncompletion, Lenz, Miller, and E. Katz each offer solid support for the relationship with faculty/advisor element. Lenz found that "completers" of the Ph.D. degree were enabled by, among other things, a caring advisor; and Miller found that one of the reasons students left doctoral programs prior to completing the degree was due to the student's relationship with the advisor. Katz advocates restructuring the dissertation process to provide for more faculty support at critical stages of the process, and the infusion of more research experiences in the graduate program.

Undergraduate Students

Undergraduates have been the focus of the majority of the student developmental research. This assumption is confirmed by a review of the bibliography on academic advising by Gordon (1994). All of the articles in chapter two, "Developmental Advising," focus on undergraduates, with the exception of a few on multicultural populations and women.

In 1985, McCarthy published the often quoted essay, "The Faculty Problem." Faculty are often successful in conducting research, teaching, and publishing without the use of libraries. However, students who are not as familiar with the literature of specific subject areas must use the resources found in the library and other sources of information to complete their studies. "Without faculty encouraging their students and modeling library use, students will not be motivated to explore the wealth of information found in the library" (Morner 1993, p. 15). Postman (1979) noted that faculty are generally satisfied with the way that they carry out research and that efforts to change their research habits by librarians have not caused a change in the faculty's attitude toward their research strategy or library use.

Stoan's "Research and Library Skills: An Analysis and Interpretation" (1984) concluded that faculty are teaching students research skills, as opposed to library research skills. He continued "research skills and library skills are not the same thing nor bear any organic relationship to each other. Research skills center on the quest for knowledge; library skills center on the search for information" (p. 105). Other studies (Baxter 1990; Eichman 1979; Epp and Segal 1987; Schloman, Lilly, and Hu 1989) echo the general literature findings that faculty use as primary sources of information colleagues, personal libraries (books and journals), and bibliographies.

Morner noted that faculty, based on their defined information-seeking habits, were more likely to search for known items in a library catalog than to conduct subject or keyword searches. In Lubans's 1974 study, "Library-use instruction needs from the library users'/non users' point of view," showed that the teaching faculty directly affects the students' use or non-use of the library. If faculty are not frequent users of the library, they tend not to stress to their students the importance of library usage in completing their assignments (p. 18).

Amstutz and Whitson (1997) conducted a descriptive study on faculty and academic professors which asked how they acquire information and how they encourage students to access and use information. The findings described the characteristics and roles of faculty who use technology for information access, which resources they use, which resources they promote to students, and who has the responsibility for developing students' information access skills.

It was found that faculty continue to use traditional sources, books remain the most common source for faculty needs, and textbooks remain as the resource required in classes. Fifty percent of the faculty never mentioned CD-ROM sources, 14 percent never mentioned the Internet, and 52 percent never mentioned the computer library catalog system. Although 95 percent of the faculty considered information access skills essential or very important, only 27 percent felt the faculty were important in helping students to develop these skills. Forty-five percent rely on the library to teach these skills and 64 percent place responsibility for developing information skills on students themselves.

Maio's 1995 dissertation, *The Instruction of Undergraduates in Print and Electronic Information Resources,* surveyed faculty of undergraduates (n=495) at three Connecticut institutions and found that in response to the question, "Do faculty require students to use information resources outside the textbook and lecture?" nearly 74 percent responded affirmatively; more than a quarter responded negatively (p. 78). When asked, "Do faculty instruct students in information resources in a discipline, or do they expect students to learn on their own general information-seeking methods and skills which they can apply to independent research?" more than 70 percent expected students to learn, at least partially, from a college librarian; almost 30 percent from college instructors; 21.2 percent in high school; and 20 percent expected students to learn on their own (p. 84).

When queried about information resources used in their own research, responses indicated that CD-ROMs/on-line databases were used frequently or sometimes by more than 50 percent of the sample; and rarely/never or not applicable to 46.7 percent. Reported use of Journals/Current Contents was more favorable with frequent or sometime use by 72.1 percent and 19.2 percent respectively.

When asked, "What kinds of information resources do faculty instruct students to use?" to determine "faculty involvement in promoting information literacy skills by including instruction in appropriate information resources in the curriculum" (p. 114), responses indicated that most faculty instructed students to consult authors (first), and journals (second) (p. 149); and more than half do not tell students about electronic mail and discussion lists (p. 150).

Nowakowski and Frick (1995) hypothesized that faculty attitudes toward information literacy, their disciplinary inclinations, their own background, and experience with information, are variables that affect the transmission of information literacy skills to students. They conducted a survey of faculty in all disciplines and found that, in general, there is a great deal of faculty support for student information literacy. The authors found that 97.6 percent of the faculty that responded to the survey agreed that undergraduates should know how to do library research and 99.5 percent of those agreed that these skills (able to find information efficiently) would be essential to students later in life. About 72 percent of the faculty agreed they themselves did not have enough time to handle their teaching loads and library research skills and only 62.3 percent of those responding included library use in the design of their coursework.

The authors also found that more than 91 percent of the faculty agreed librarians and faculty should be partners in the educational process, and nearly 92 percent agreed that a requirement of the undergraduate degree should be learning how to do library research.

Nowakowski and Frick based their questionnaire on one developed by Hardesty in his 1982 doctoral dissertation, *The Development of a Set of Scales to Measure the Attitudes of Classroom Instructors toward the Undergraduate Educational Role of the Academic Library*, where he discovered a correlation between the attitudes of classroom instructors and the role of the academic library in the instructor population.

Maynard (1990) conducted a study of the teaching faculty at a military college to learn how the English faculty compared to other faculty and also of their attitudes toward library instruction. He believed that librarians needed the cooperation of the teaching faculty more than ever now that "with the advances in technology, electronic library literacy has become more crucial . . . these advances have created more obstacles to student competency in information retrieval" (p. 67).

Maynard found that 68 percent of all faculty responded that they had learned their library skills on their own. Approximately 81 percent of the professors who responded affirmatively to the question "Do you offer library instruction to your students?" had learned library skills on their own. Although most of the faculty agreed that library instruction was important, less than 17 percent felt they should provide it. Also, more than half of the faculty (53 percent) had never requested class-related instruction from librarians. When queried, some admitted having no knowledge of its availability.

Lubans (1980), in a faculty survey at a four-year institution, reported that 30 percent of the responses to the question "Who is responsible for students learning library skills?" indicated the English department. Although Maynard's case study did not find significant differences between the English faculty and faculty in other disciplines, he found that more than 75 percent of the English faculty and 40 percent of other faculty agreed that both librarians and teachers should be responsible for library instruction. He also found that 10 percent of all faculty felt that their students needed library instruction and 94 percent of all faculty believed library instruction was important; however, the "faculty gave lukewarm support to the idea of helping design and use new methods" (p. 71).

Kohl's *Reference Services and Library Instruction* (1985), a summary of quantitative research, verifies Thomas's ("Faculty Attitudes and Habits Concerning Library Instruction," 1994) later observation that "there ha[d] been little exploration of the teaching attitudes toward instructional efforts of their colleagues in the library." In 1994, J. Thomas replicated a 1982 study she conducted with Ensor ("The University Faculty and Library Instruction") in which it was revealed the faculty believed that students should learn library skills on their own. She reported that in general, the faculty still feel little responsibility for ensuring students develop library skills, traditional or electronic. A large number (41.1 percent) still believe students learn on their own.

Cannon's 1994 "Faculty Survey on Library Research Instruction," (n=229), found that "faculty from all departments overwhelmingly agreed that library research is important in their fields" (p. 526). Cannon also reported that when faculty were asked to rate the abilities of their first- and second-year students to do library research using a five-point Likert type scale (no opinion, poor, satisfactory, good, or very good), 70 percent rated the students' ability as poor. More than half the faculty (52 percent) gave a rating of satisfactory to third- and fourth-year students, and for graduate students, 48 percent rated them as good. Few students received a rating of "very good" leading Cannon to speculate that "This suggests that a majority of faculty feel their students learn library research skills over the years. However, given that at no level did the students rate a majority response of 'very good,' it is obvious that faculty see considerable room for improvement" (p. 528).

Haws, Peterson, and Shonrock (1989) surveyed faculty attitudes toward a library skills course and found the following:

- 70 percent believed incoming freshmen do not have the necessary skills to use a research library;
- 88 percent believed that it is important for college students to know how to use the library;
- 62 percent believed a library skills course should be required of undergraduates;
- 22 percent indicated that bibliographic instruction was an integral part of their course objectives;
- 10 percent use library faculty to present course objectives. (p. 202)

In 1993, Nowakowski reported that a recent survey of faculty attitudes revealed there was a strong faculty support for information literacy skills. Arp and Wilson ("Structures of Bibliographic Instruction Programs," 1989), Arp and Kenny ("Vital Connections: Composition and BI Theory in the LRC," 1990), and Lowe ("Collaboration with Faculty: Integrating Information Literacy into the Curriculum,"1995) all discuss cooperation with teaching faculty in the teaching and provision of information skills, and Breivik ("Politics for Closing the Gap," 1989) advocates more involvement of librarians in the instructional process to help bring about quality education for the information age.

Cooper and Burchfield (1995) viewed information literacy in a different way and explored the advantages and disadvantages of offering information literacy programs to college and university staff and the feasibility of integrating these sessions into the workplace; and Werrell and Wesley (1990) describe a faculty development workshop that was designed to provide a forum for improving library research assignments and to promote information literacy.

Relevance

This section will discuss the attitudinal literature on college-level students and information literacy skills. It also includes the limited data available on students' levels of performance when tested for skills in evaluation. It is presumed, for the purposes of this research, that the attitudinal and performance components of information literacy skills, are correlated and are predictors of relevance.

Role of Attitude

The research that has been conducted on the attitudes of college-level students about information literacy is limited and includes only one study conducted on undergraduates. Information literacy survey instruments developed by Maughan (1994) and Daragan and Stevens (1996) did not include a section on attitudes. There is a large body of literature on attitudes about library research skills, however, it will not be addressed here. Some of the results of these types of studies are presented in the preceding sections on exposure, experience, and relationship with faculty/advisor where relevant. There is no research currently, on graduate student populations on attitude or performance.

Undergraduate Students

H. Morrison's 1997 exploratory study of undergraduate students, "Information Literacy Skills: An Exploratory Focus Group Study of Student Perceptions" (n=7), was conducted "to explore the students' thoughts on information literacy and ways for libraries to contribute to the development of information literacy skills" (p. 5). The group responded to four main information literacy skills—recognizing a need for information, locating information, evaluating information, and effectively using information.

The students unanimously agreed that "locating information" was a skill, however, they disagreed as to whether "recognizing a need for information" was a skill. H. Morrison reported that at least one of the participants strongly felt that "anyone can recognize a need for information." The other students felt there was an art to recognizing this need, "perhaps the attributes of curiosity or open-mindedness." The researcher noted that one reason for the lack of identification of this concept as a skill may stem from "feelings of anxiety associated with the initial stages of information seeking." She cited Kuhlthau's 1993 study of high school seniors, *Seeking Meaning: A Process Approach to Library and Information Services*, which found six stages of information seeking. Four of these six occur before the information collecting begin. Kuhlthau's first and third stages, task initiation and prefocus exploration, are typical in that they are accompanied by feelings of uncertainty and apprehension, confusion, uncertainty, and doubt respectively. H. Morrison concluded

> The frequency with which participants in the focus group referred to attitudinal/emotional factors, and the emphasis placed on positive experiences with library staff, particularly in the initial stages of learning to use a library, support the view that recognizing a need for information may produce anxiety.

> Perhaps, then, recognizing a need for information is not a skill per se, but an attitudinal/emotional component of information literacy. That is, the information literate person, on discovering a need for information, is able to deal with the emotional aspect and go on to the next stage, gathering information. (p. 11)

The group was also unanimous in agreeing that the most advanced skill of the four was "evaluating information" and included the following skills as a part of this process: currency, credibility, relevance, originality, and the time required to use it (p. 7). It should also be noted that the group itself expressed a lack of confidence in their ability to evaluate information, citing credibility specifically. The group was less than unanimous in their agreement about the "effectiveness of using information" as a skill. H. Morrison reports that their discussion focused on the meaning of effective use of information and included issues such as formatting, plagiarizing, creating an original work, and the impact of the information on the reader (p. 7).

The author concluded that the results of the study showed that undergraduates do feel that information literacy is a valuable skill, and also, "believe that a certain level of information literacy skill should be attained in the course of pursuing an undergraduate degree." She suggested that more work be done to define what constitutes information literacy as a result of the students' discussion of the meaning of recognizing a need for information. She also suggested that in considering the informational needs of students, their emotional needs should be addressed as well, paying particular attention to library anxiety (p. 13).

Role of Performance

It is not surprising that the beginning attempts at information literacy assessment include librarians and library media specialists. Academic librarians have developed guides on, for, and about information literacy, as well as numerous programs and courses, but there have been few published attempts to measure the outcomes of these endeavors. Maughan, the user research coordinator at the University of California (UC), Berkeley Teaching Library, is conducting ongoing empirical research via the distribution of an information literacy survey to graduating seniors. The survey, "The Teaching Library-Information Literacy Survey," (1994) is believed to be the largest of its kind (n=255), and was conducted to "better understand and document the library skills acquired by graduating seniors in the Political Science and Sociology departments during the course of their studies at UC Berkeley."

Before the survey, students were asked to self-rate library skills (excellent, pretty good, fair, pretty poor), if they had taken any library instruction at UC, and if so, how much, and how many research papers they had written as undergraduates. Although 93 percent of the students surveyed perceived their library skills as fair, pretty good, or excellent, and only 7 percent rated their skills as pretty poor, 63 percent received poor to failing scores on the survey, and less than 2 percent scored 90 percent or higher.

Maughan reports that "A question-by-question review of the responses revealed that fewer than 50 percent of the respondents were able to properly search for library materials by subject, correctly identify citations to books and journal articles, limit online search results by language, recognize and identify key reference sources in the social sciences, or recognize and identify key electronic sources in their subject major." The closest items to testing evaluation skills on Maughan's information literacy instrument were items which tested the ability to correctly identify citations from books and journal articles.

In 1996, Orr, Appleton, and Andrews described an interactive workshop to facilitate teaching information literacy skills to remote students. Although one of the program objectives was "to encourage students to develop critical evaluation skills" (p. 229), a discussion of the two-day program provided no reference to teaching evaluation skills (p. 230).

Daragan and Stevens (1996) used an integrative and developmental approach to information literacy. They constructed a test in "Developing Lifelong Learners: An Integrative and Developmental Approach to Information Literacy," to be used with their four-year course integrated library instruction program for a military institution, based on Perry's (1970) developmental model. Although the authors defined information literacy as "knowing when one needs information, where to find information, how to evaluate information, and how to use information in decision making and problem solving," (p. 69) the four test sections in the instrument were identified as indexes and abstracts; on-line capabilities; research strategy skills; and Library of Congress classification skills (p. 74).

The authors used the instrument as a pre- and post-test measure (p. 74) and reported the following: For section one (indexes and abstracts), with a possible highest score of thirty-three, pre-test percentages correct were 74.2, and post-test scores increased to 78.5 percent. For section two (on-line capabilities—highest score of twenty-six), pre-test percentages correct were 62.3, and post-test increased to 70.4 percent. There was very little change in the research strategies section—highest possible score of nine, with the pre-test percentage correct as 42.2, and post-test increased to 43.3 percent. The last section, Library of Congress classifications—with the highest possible score of six—reported pre-test percentages correct at 68.3 percent, and post-test percentages increasing to 73.3 percent (pp. 76-77). Data analysis revealed the results supported two broad conclusions:

1. [Our] in-class, across-the-curriculum intervention succeeded in increasing student levels of information literacy; and
2. Levels of information literacy among in-coming students vary widely, and that variance is decreased slightly after a semester of integrated library instruction. (p. 75)

In "Things They Carry: Attitudes toward, Opinions about, and Knowledge of Libraries and Research among Incoming College Students" (1998), Geffert and Christensen found that when asked about their (n=521) self-reported comfort levels in their ability to evaluate whether the information sources they found were relevant, 87 percent reported being very or somewhat comfortable in doing so; and 12.9 percent reported being somewhat uncomfortable or very uncomfortable. When asked about comfort levels in evaluating the literature cited in the author's arguments, 65.3 percent reported feeling very or somewhat comfortable; 34.7 percent reported feeling somewhat or very uncomfortable. When asked to compare, in general, the reliability of books and articles from an academic library to material found on the Internet, responses indicated that 6.4 percent found information on the Internet more reliable; 60.3 percent found it equally reliable; and only 31.3 percent found it less reliable (pp. 287-88). Overall, the researchers concluded that there appeared "to be little relationship between self-confidence and knowledge of several basic library concepts" (p. 283).

Research with Information Literacy Component

A review of the literature reveals there are several studies which claim to include a component of information literacy. Examples include previously discussed research by Libutti (1991) and Ochs et al. (1991), however, neither study correlated their definition of information literacy with their interpretation of information literacy skills.

South Seattle Community College (1993) included an information literacy component in their library user survey. The questions the authors asked to get some measure of information literacy included: how they most often located materials in the library (45 percent computer catalog; 29 percent asked staff; 5 percent asked fellow students; 22 percent browsed or located materials in some other way; 20 percent used interlibrary loan); had a library card from a public library (73 percent); if they had taken a library techniques class (45 percent); had library orientation through one of their classes (45 percent); read magazines to keep current about their fields (42 percent); used library materials to find information about careers (41 percent); used either a print or computerized periodical index to find magazine articles (52 percent); and used a newspaper index to find a newspaper article (34 percent). The authors concluded

> When information literacy variables are broken down by library usage it becomes clear that people who use the library more are more information literate than those who don't. Whether frequent library usage leads to information literacy or information literacy leads to frequent library use is not possible to tell by the data . . . specific training in the use of the library, either through a library techniques class or an orientation offered as part of another class, definitely promotes information literacy. (p. 10)

This conclusion would be correct if the authors had correctly identified information literacy skills as opposed to library use statistics.

Recognizing the lack of a tool to assess the development of research competencies, Geffert and Bruce (1997) conducted a longitudinal study to measure graduating seniors' research competencies and opinions after four years of course-integrated library instruction. In "Whither BI?" students were asked to indicate if they felt "very comfortable" "somewhat comfortable," "somewhat uncomfortable," or "very uncomfortable," and also to identify persons, including themselves, from whom they had learned various research skills and tools; to evaluate their comfort level with each item; to identify courses in which they received bibliographic instruction; and rate the usefulness of their first two sessions. Three open-ended questions were included which asked students to identify problems they face when conducting research, and how or if bibliographic instruction helped them to address these problems.

In looking at the variables studied which represent information literacy skills, the researchers found 98.6 percent reported they were comfortable with the on-line catalog and 86.5 percent were comfortable in their ability to choose appropriate research materials; 75.5 percent felt very or somewhat comfortable in evaluating the authority of resources, but only 36.1 percent of these felt very comfortable. Almost 88 percent felt very or somewhat comfortable in evaluating the relevance of sources, but only 45.8 percent of those felt very comfortable. Students also rated their own abilities on nine out of eleven skills higher than when they had learned part of the skills in a bibliographic instruction session.

Note

1. *ERIC* is the U.S. Department of Education Educational Resource Information Center database. See http://askeric.org/Eric/.

Chapter 4

Research Findings and Summary

Introduction

This section presents the findings of the study descriptively and analytically including the testing of the model. The demographic section will be discussed first, followed by the findings for each of the elements: exposure, experience, relationship with faculty, attitude, and performance. Discussion of findings for the relevance section are also included along with discussion and statistical analysis of the model, testing of the model, and additional statistical analysis between groups allowing for gender and academic status. Undergraduates and graduate students will be discussed together and in cases when it is statistically significant, findings will be presented separately for each group.

Because the survey instrument was automated and appeared to the student participants as seven separate World Wide Web pages via the Netscape™ browser, the total sample number for each section is different as shown in table 4.1. Due to human testing regulations at the Targeted University, students in the population could not be required to take and complete the survey. The first page of the Neely Test, the letter distributed to the faculty, and the letter to the students, for recruitment purposes, all informed the students of their rights in participating in the research study and included the following statement:[1]

> Participation in this research is voluntary and once you have decided to participate, you may withdraw consent and stop participating at any time without penalty or loss of any benefits.

This statement, and the fact some participants may have inadvertently skipped some sections and/or items, may have contributed to the lack of continuity in survey section completion numbers. After eliminating duplicate records, where it appeared participants used the Back button of the Netscape browser, thereby remitting a set of data more than once, the final totals were attained.

Table 4.1. Completed Survey Sections

Model Elements	Total Records per Section
Exposure	N=144
Attitude	N=141
Relationship With Faculty	N=140
Performance	N=139
Experience	N=139
Relevance	N=141
Demographics	N=136

Throughout this discussion of study findings, percentages for each section are based on total number of records per section. No percentage totals are rounded up or down. Null or unanswered items are presented only when statistically significant. For example, the experience section is the only section that asked questions which had one correct answer for each item. For this particular section, the number of items answered incorrectly plus the number unanswered produced the total number incorrect.

Descriptive Statistics

Demographics

Because the study was designed to elicit information from students at three academic levels—undergraduate, master's, and doctoral—the demographic section of the Morner Test was used with minimal adaptation.

Gender and Age

The total sample (N=136) is comprised of forty-six males and eighty-six females. Four participants left this item blank. The age distribution is depicted in table 4.2. Nearly 45 percent of the participants reported their age as falling within the "21 to 25" age group. This number is consistent with the majority of the sample (61.76 percent) currently being enrolled in a master's program or as seniors in an undergraduate program. More than 15 percent of the sample fall into the nontraditional student category, above age thirty-one.

Table 4.2. Age of population

N=136	Age categories	Percentage of Total
28	18-20	20.58
61	21-25	44.85
23	26-30	16.91
7	31-35	05.14
15	Above 35	11.02

Current Academic Status

The current academic status of students in the sample is shown in table 4.3. More than 60 percent of the sample is made up of master's students and seniors in the undergraduate population (n=84).

Table 4.3. Current Academic Status

N=136	Academic Status	Percentage of Total
5	Freshman	03.67
16	Sophomore	11.76
19	Junior	13.97
33	Senior	24.46
51	Masters	37.50
3	Doctoral	02.20
7	Other	05.14

The total number of undergraduates comprise more than half of the population or 53.67 percent. Unfortunately, the numbers of doctoral participants and freshman in the sample are extremely low, and this may prohibit the ability to compare these students to master's students and other undergraduates in this study with any statistically generalizable results.

Item "g" or the "other" category was selected by seven participants who listed post bachelor (three), teacher licensure (one), guest scholar program (one), and postgraduate in teacher licensure program but applying to graduate school (one). One individual did not indicate an answer in the "other" column.

Undergraduate Major

An undergraduate major or previous undergraduate work was indicated by all but four of the respondents. Thirty-five of those responding selected "social science" as the area of their undergraduate work. Twenty-one selected "education," and "humanities, visual and performing arts," respectively. Fourteen students selected "math/science," and thirteen selected "business." Twenty-eight students selected item "f" or the "other" category, and an additional three individuals did not select item "f" but typed in an answer in the "other" category.

Current Academic Program

Table 4.4 shows the data collected on the academic program students were currently enrolled in. Thirty-four or 25 percent of those surveyed selected "other," as their current academic program was not listed in the choices given. This may be contributed to the need to further diversify the sample and the inclusion of students from a non-core Education course (ET 200). Nearly 30 percent of those surveyed responded that "higher education, education administration, policy studies, or planning" was their current academic program.

Table 4.4. Current Academic Program

N=136	Academic Program	Percentage Selected
40	Higher education, etc.	29.41
5	Educational research	03.67
21	Instruction or Curriculum	15.44
22	Counseling, educational psychology, or developmental psychology	16.17
1	Special education	00.73
34	Other	25.00

Experience in Libraries—Anxiety

Frustration and library anxiety are commonly recognized occurrences that are well represented in the library science and education literature (see Keefer 1993; Kuhlthau 1988, 1991, 1993; Mellon 1986; H. Morrison 1997; M. J. Rudd and J. Rudd 1986a; J. Rudd and M. J. Rudd 1986b). Mech and Brooks' 1995 quantitative study of 153 college students reported that library anxiety "was found to be a different condition from the general psychological trait of anxiety" (p. 175). In their study, library anxiety scores were consistently higher in all respondents than trait anxiety scores (p. 176).

As a result of the preliminary research conducted to develop the Morner (1993) instrument (Morner Test) to measure the library skills of doctoral education students, Morner found that library frustration was a problem and, therefore, included it as a test item in her instrument. However, the purpose of her dissertation was to develop and validate the instrument, and so, specific findings for the demographic item depicting frustration, from which the current survey item sixty-four was directly adopted, were not reported.

Of the one hundred and thirty-six individuals responding to the demographic section of this survey, 83.82 percent responded affirmatively when asked about library frustration. Nearly 70 percent of the sample selected response b—"I can usually find what I want but there are frustrations," and almost 16 percent selected item c—"Libraries are a frustrating place; I find it difficult to find the information I need." Of those twenty-one selecting item c, four were sophomores, six were juniors, two were seniors, eight were master's students, and one a doctoral student. Only 11.76 percent responded that "Whenever I use the library I find what I want," and five persons (3 master's, 1 senior, and 1 other) indicated that "I generally avoid libraries, preferring to use personal, faculty loaned or departmental collections for research purposes." These findings are consistent with the few research studies that have been conducted on library anxiety (Kuhlthau 1983, 1989, 1991; Mellon 1986).

Mellon's (1986) qualitative study of 6,000 undergraduate students (primarily freshmen) in beginning composition courses over a period of two years found that "75 to 85 percent of students in each class described their initial response to the library in terms of fear or anxiety" (p. 162). Mellon's findings led to the formulation of a grounded theory in library anxiety.

When confronted with the need to gather information in the library for their first research paper many students become so anxious that they are unable to approach the problem logically or effectively. (p. 163)

Mellon compared her findings with work being done in math anxiety and concluded that library anxiety should be treated within the anxiety framework by "acknowledging the anxiety and its legitimacy, and then providing successful experiences to counteract the anxiety." She continued and noted that the literature revealed this was the most effective method for treatment (p. 163).

Kuhlthau's (1983) research of "twenty-six academically capable high school seniors," which led to the model of the information search process (ISP), identified anxiety during the task initiation (recognize a need for information), topic selection (identify and select the general topic to be investigated or the approach to be pursued), and prefocus exploration (investigate information on the general topic in order to extend personal understanding) stages (Kuhlthau 1991, p. 366).

Although Kuhlthau's initial research was conducted on secondary school students, additional testing of the ISP model (Kuhlthau 1989) of 385 academic, public, and school library users at 21 sites revealed similar results. "The adjectives most used to describe feelings were confused, frustrated, and doubtful at initiation" (Kuhlthau 1989, p. 21).

Library Anxiety and the Neely Test

During the pilot test of the Neely Test of Relevance, Evaluation, and Information Literacy Attitudes (Neely Test),[2] comments about survey length and that it "felt like a test" prompted the researcher to make the act of making the library-related survey as positive and anxiety-free as possible. As a result, the following measures were undertaken:

1. The acquisition of a choice of gifts for survey participants—participants were offered their choice of a stuffed Cam the Ram (the mascot of the Targeted University); Five one dollar Walrus™ Dollars (from a popular local ice-cream parlor); or, a key chain (lanyard) with a wide ribbon (emblazoned with the Targeted University's colors and initials) designed to be worn around the neck. The Ram and ice cream dollars were the most popular gifts.
2. The use of the researcher's nephew's likeness at nineteen months old with an enormous afro on the opening page of the survey. This elicited many smiles and laughter.

3. The use of a banner [scrolling mechanism] in the Netscape browser during the Attitude section of the survey at the bottom of the screen which read "Walrus Ice Cream . . . Yum Yum!!!!!"

4. The use of a cartoon walrus reminding participants that "ice cream sure tastes good" halfway through the survey instrument in the Performance section.

5. The use of a banner [scrolling mechanism] in the Netscape browser during the Experience section of the survey at the bottom of the screen which read, "Relax, you're not being graded for this one!!" This elicited smiles and laughter as well.

6. The final page of the automated survey was in pale pastel colors, and included the likeness of a huge ice cream cone and the Targeted University's bookstore's initials (the stuffed Cam and the key chain were acquired from the University bookstore) and the following: Thank you very much for participating in this survey. See Teresa for a Thank you and a surprize!!!

7. The researcher was present during the testing of all students with the exception of a few and took the opportunity to thank the participants for their participation before and after test completion, to remind them that it was not a test, that there was no way to connect the individual with the answers after test completion, and that all responses were completely anonymous.

Testing the Instrument—Test Time Completion

An important part of this study, along with data analysis, is the testing of the survey instrument. The automated instrument resided on a server on the library network at the researcher's home university and each time a survey was completed, the total time from when the participant began until test completion was recorded based on the program written and the time mechanism on the network server. Due to circumstances beyond the control of the researcher, times were not recorded for more than half the population (65.44 percent or 89 participants). Actual times recorded ranged from one hundred to fifteen minutes with a mean time of nearly thirty-one minutes (30.78). An average (mean) time of almost thirty-nine (38.4) minutes was recorded for volunteers who provided test data for database creation and testing by taking the test manually, and the undergraduate, master's and Ph.D. students who provided input for instrument construction during the pilot had a mean time of nearly thirty-nine minutes (38.42). It appears that the automated instrument version reduced the mean test taking time by nearly eight minutes, in comparison with the manual paper and pen format.

Computer Use

Survey participants were asked to respond about their general use of computers, and were allowed to select all answers that were applicable. Nearly 89 percent of the participants reported that they used computers for "E-mail/Chat rooms," almost 90 percent used computers for "Word processing/Spreadsheets," and a little more than 88 percent used computers for the "Internet/World Wide Web." It is promising for libraries and information service providers to note that nearly 73 percent of those responding reported that they "Search databases." General computer use for the entire sample can be found in table B.1, appendix B.

There was no Morner demographic item with which to compare the data from this query. This item was adapted from Morner item 6 to allow for specific computer use. For item 66, which asked about the participants use of computers in libraries, one hundred and twenty-six of the respondents reported that they had used computers in libraries. Only nine reported that they had not.

The final item in the demographic section asked about the comfort level in using library databases. This item, along with item 66, was adapted from Morner item 8 to allow for more clarity. Seventy-seven (51.47 percent) of the respondents reported that their experience was comfortable with library databases, a finding that appears to be in contrast with the large number of participants (83.82 percent) who reported feeling frustrated with libraries. There apparently must be another aspect of the library environment which contributes to library anxiety rather than library databases. More than a quarter of the respondents answered that they feel uncomfortable or very uncomfortable with library databases, and only thirteen reported that they feel very comfortable.

Summary

This section presented descriptive statistics on data collected in the demographic section of the survey. More than two thirds of the sample (n=136) is female and the remainder male. The majority of the sample age falls within the "21 to 25" age group (61), and fifteen respondents fall into the nontraditional student age group of "above 35." Undergraduate seniors (33) and master's level students (51) make up the bulk of the group tested, and undergraduates make up more than half of the sample (73) with five freshmen, sixteen sophomores, nineteen juniors and thirty-three seniors. There are only three doctoral students in the sample.

There were no discerning patterns in the undergraduate majors of the sample, although it should be noted that "social science" and 'humanities, visual and performing arts" were both selected by significant percentages of the sample at thirty-five and twenty-one individuals respectively. The current academic program item revealed forty of the participants are currently enrolled in "higher education, education administration, policy studies, or planning," thirty-four selected the "other" category, twenty-two selected "counseling, educational psychology, or developmental psychology," and twenty-one are enrolled in programs focusing on "instruction or curriculum."

More than 70 percent of those participating revealed that they can usually find what they want in libraries but there are frustrations, confirming that library anxiety is a common problem at all levels that must be addressed. In contrast, only sixteen persons reported that they find what they want whenever they use the library. As to be expected, with the current increased focus on technology, nearly 93 percent of those responding revealed that they use computers in libraries and almost 57 percent reported their experience with library computer databases as comfortable. Nearly 10 percent revealed their experiences to be very comfortable and more than a quarter responded that their experiences were either uncomfortable or very uncomfortable with library databases.

The mean time for completing the automated instrument was almost thirty-one minutes, nearly eight minutes less than times recorded for manual completion.

Participants revealed that they use computers in general for a variety of reasons including "Word processing/Spreadsheets" (122), "E-mail/Chat rooms" (121), "Internet/World Wide Web" (120) and "Searching databases" (99). The use of computers for "Games/Entertainment" (75), and "Work-related/Telecommuting" (39) was less prevalent.

The next section will discuss findings from data collected for the predicting performance and attitudinal aspect of the model (see figure 3.2).

Predicting Performance and Attitude

Using descriptive statistics this section will present the findings which correspond to the model's predicting performance and attitude variables. It will include findings for the entire sample on exposure, relationship with faculty, and experience.

Role of Exposure

The first eight questions in the exposure section requested information about different types of library orientation, "currently," since the beginning of the academic program the respondent was currently enrolled in, and "in general," throughout their academic careers. In nearly every section there was compelling evidence which shows that participants have had either no exposure to the library environment or have only been exposed minimally, "1 to 2 times." Tables 4.5 and 4.6 show detailed findings for this section.

In thirteen of the sixteen scenarios, currently and in general, more than 50 percent of those responding reported that they had had no exposure to the library. In nine of those thirteen scenarios, more than 60 percent reported no exposure. In comparing the undergraduate students in the sample to the graduate students, more than 50 percent of the undergraduates and nearly 45 percent of the graduate students reported having no exposure.

The number of participants reporting no exposure (0 times) "In general" is significant because the numbers are large in the categories that were reported by Toomer (1993) as preferable for adult learners (see tables 4.5 and 4.6, numbers 5, 6, and 8). This could also be a function of Toomer's conclusion that these "self-learning methodologies" are not being "utilized effectively" by librarians and information professionals (pp. 81-82).

In comparison with Morner's (1993) findings on a similar item, almost 39 percent of Morner's 144 doctoral students reported no instruction at all. Nearly 26 percent of those in the current study reported no "library instruction as a part of a class," and 81 percent reported no "library instruction course for credit." Morner's additional exposure findings are not readily comparable to the findings of this study, however, the current study provides a snapshot of a detailed view of the samples' exposure in eight categories, currently and historically. This researcher was unable to find any published empirical evidence that explored exposure in such detail, and as a result, the findings of this study are also not readily comparable to previously reported research. However, the data presented here provides further illumination upon previously reported studies of graduate populations by Alire (1984), Farid et al. (1984), Libutti (1991), Parrish (1989a, 1989b), Simon (1995), and Thaxton (1985). Research by Damko (1990), Geffert and Bruce (1997), and Maughan (1994) focused on undergraduate populations. All reported low exposure from significant portions of their respective samples.

Table 4.5. Exposure—In General

	0 Times		1-2 Times		3-4 Times		5-6 Times		7 or More Times	
	N=144	%	N=144	%	N=144	%	N=144	%	N=144	%
1. Tour/orientation	45	31.25	60	41.66	13	09.020	6	4.16	9	6.25
2. Instruction/class	37	25.69	61	42.36	21	14.580	2	1.38	10	6.94
3. Workshop in library	63	43.75	45	31.25	13	09.020	2	1.38	7	4.86
4. One-on-one with librarian	82	56.94	30	20.83	11	07.630	4	2.77	0	—
5. Course for credit	116	80.55	13	09.02	1	00.694	0	—	0	—
6. Self-guided tour	31	21.52	48	33.33	32	22.220	5	3.47	8	5.55
7. Small group training	73	50.69	41	28.47	7	04.860	4	2.77	5	3.47
8. Tutorials	78	54.16	33	22.91	9	06.250	4	2.77	4	2.77

Table 4.6. Exposure—Currently

| | 0 Times | | 1-2 Times | | 3-4 Times | | 5-6 Times | | 7 or More Times | |
	N=144	%	N=144	%	N=144	%	N=144	%	N=144	%
1. Tour/orientation	82	56.94	42	29.16	9	06.25	1	0.694	1	0.694
2. Instruction/class	71	49.30	53	36.80	8	05.55	2	1.380	1	0.694
3. Workshop in library	81	56.25	46	31.94	4	02.77	2	1.380	1	0.694
4. One-on-one with librarian	106	73.61	22	15.27	4	02.77	0	—	0	—
5. Course for credit	127	88.19	4	02.77	2	01.38	0	—	0	—
6. Self-guided tour	72	50.00	42	29.16	16	11.11	1	0.694	3	2.080
7. Small group training	94	65.27	35	24.30	3	02.08	1	0.694	0	—
8. Tutorials	91	63.19	28	19.44	8	05.55	4	2.770	2	1.380

With the exception of the nearly 39 percent reporting no exposure (instruction), other Morner (1993) results in this category are also not readily comparable to the current dissertation findings as a result of her categorizations. Morner items 9 through 12 were adapted for the Neely Test and additional exposure categories were added. Findings for these items are consistent with previously reported research by Farid et al. (1984), Geffert and Bruce (1997), Libutti (1991), Parrish (1989), Simon (1995), Thaxton (1985), and Toomer (1993) who each reported on either undergraduate or graduate students and the limited amount of instruction and orientation they had been exposed to.

In his 1993 dissertation, Toomer reported in his conclusions that "The research and professional literature all suggested that self-learning methodologies for instructional delivery have not yet been utilized effectively, especially computer and other electronic multi-media technology" (p. 82). It is difficult to determine, from the current data, whether Toomer's 1993 assertions still hold true. The findings in the current study for the total sample, at least "1 to 2 times," in terms of self-learning methodologies (defined in this study as library instruction course for credit [#5], self-guided tours [#6], and automated tutorials [#8]) appear to be low when compared to the totals for the more traditional methods of bibliographic instruction such as orientation, library instruction as part of a class or a lecture, or workshop in the library. The total sample number who have engaged in these activities currently is 2.77 percent (library instruction for credit), 29.16 percent (self-guided tour), and 19.44 percent (automated tutorials). In general totals are slightly higher at 9.02 percent, 33.33 percent, and 22.91 percent, respectively. The methodologies and sample populations of both the current study and Toomer's study prohibit the ability to compare quantitative findings on preferred adult learner preferences for bibliographic instruction; however, the data provided by the current study provides significant baseline data, in terms of the current sample numbers, for comparing empirical data from which Toomer's assertions might be further examined. For example, the nearly 23 percent of the current sample who have used automated tutorials "1 to 2 times," in general, can be interpreted as correlating to the increasing use of electronic resources which include on-line tutorials, and also, those practitioners who develop their own tutorials (see Buntrock 1988; Courtois 1991; James 1986; Leach 1993; Markley and Stein 1998; Nickerson 1991; Tennant 1998).

The Usefulness of Formal Library Instruction

Thirty-four percent of the survey participants who had engaged in formal library instruction reported it was helpful, nearly 16 percent reported that it was extremely helpful, and 15.27 percent reported that it was somewhat helpful. These findings provide evidence to support the notion that the minimum level of exposure, or participation in any exposure category, "1 to 2 times," is considered helpful by survey participants. Almost 23 percent reported that they had not had formal library instruction. Three of the respondents reported that formal library instruction was not helpful. Since "formal library instruction" was not defined in the Neely Test, it is not possible, from the current data, to determine how the respondents defined it in terms of their responses for items 1 through 8.

First Library Use

In research previously reported, it was noted that the two most popular and documented ways undergraduates reported learning to use the library were in high school and by self-teaching (see Damko 1990; Simon 1995). In 1984, Alire found that nearly one half of her sample (doctoral students) (48 percent) selected high school as the third highest way that doctoral education students learned to use the library. The data presented here confirms those findings. Of the 144 participants responding to the exposure section, 42, nearly 30 percent, learned to use the library on their own, and 41 learned to use the library in high school. Twenty-seven (18.75 percent) reported via the "other" category that they learned to use the library in either elementary, grammar, or grade school. Fourteen learned to use the library in college as either a part of freshman orientation (4), as part of another course (8), or as a separate course (2).

It should be noted that almost 23 percent selected the 'other' category in reporting how they first learned to use the library, and some individuals selected an item other than the "other" category and also wrote in an answer in the "other" column. Of those writing in the "other" space, two learned to use the library in middle school, four were taught by their parents, and one each learned in the public library, with a friend, as a research assistant, and as a child by a librarian. One each reported that they learned at the intermediate level (presumably equal to secondary school), was taught by her husband, learned in another country (Saudi Arabia), and worked at a college library. One individual reported that he or she had had training in the library throughout their education with the exception of graduate school.

Role of Experience

The experience section of this study was the only section which contained items which had one correct answer. With the exception of the demographic section, all other sections elicited data on the respondents perception of a particular research or information situation. Findings in this area revealed a widespread lack of knowledge about leading education resources, the publication cycle in education, and searching mechanisms. These findings clearly corroborate research previously reported by Farid et al. (1984), Libutti (1991), Morner (1993), and Thaxton (1985), that graduate students are not familiar with the resources in their subject areas, and library knowledge is greatly varied. Findings on undergraduates in the current study confirms research by Reed (1974) and York et al. (1988), which found that students are still unable to describe or identify the purpose of computerized tools, including the on-line catalog, and there is still evidence that they seem poorly skilled in the use of a college library.

The experience section was adapted almost entirely from the Morner Test. This section contained sixteen questions, each of which had one correct answer. "I don't know" was added to each item ("e" in all cases except item 57 where it is 'f') to reduce the possibility of guessing. No student answered all sixteen questions correctly. Two individuals answered eleven items correctly, and the lowest score recorded for this section was zero. Table 4.7 shows the data in detail including percentages for incorrect items, where the "Key" column is the correct answer for that item. The significant percentages recorded in the "I don't know" (E/F) column(s) revealed the overall lack of education subject knowledge, and, confirmed specific findings in experience research reported earlier by Hernandez (1985), Morner (1993), and Thaxton (1985).

In nearly 38 percent of the items in this section, 40 percent or more of the 139 responding reported they did not know the answer. Those queries included identifying a refereed journal, identifying the source least likely to aid in evaluating author credentials, knowledge of how the *ERIC* database is constructed, how to identify recent follow-up research for a key article written in 1982, how to locate reviews of published tests, and how to select subject terms used in the on-line catalog. Table 4.7 also shows in comparison to the items where the answer "I don't know" was significant, the corresponding correct item (in **bold**) was selected by only a few of the respondents, except in the case of the refereed journal (item 43), where 26.61 percent (37) selected the correct item.

Table 4.7. Experience

Test Items	Key	Percent Choosing (N=139)					
		A	B	C	D	E	F
43	C	02.15	12.94	**26.61**	05.88	49.64	
44	C	33.09	00.71	**02.87**	53.23	07.19	
45	A	**62.58**	10.79	03.59	09.35	10.07	
46	D	11.51	17.26	05.75	**25.17**	36.69	
47	D	06.47	13.66	15.82	**53.95**	06.47	
48	B	28.05	**18.70**	24.46	20.86	04.31	
49	B	23.02	**39.56**	18.70	10.79	05.03	
50	D	26.61	17.26	17.98	**24.46**	10.07	
51	C	05.75	05.03	**10.07**	33.09	43.16	
52	B	07.19	12.94	29.49	**04.31**	42.44	
53	A	**57.55**	10.79	03.59	07.91	16.54	
54	D	07.19	12.94	29.49	**04.31**	42.44	
55	C	16.54	10.07	**11.51**	02.15	55.39	
56	C	07.19	07.91	**12.94**	20.86	46.76	
57	C	07.91	06.47	**46.76**	14.38	07.91	12.94
58	D	02.87	21.58	01.43	35.97	33.09	

In reviewing individual items from this section of the survey more closely, almost 37 percent reported that they did not know the purpose of "truncation" (item 46) in a search, and an additional 34.35 percent answered this item incorrectly. Almost 62 percent (61.87 percent) answered incorrectly the item on whether an article could be evaluated for bias before it was read (item 50), nearly 46 percent (45.32 percent) did not know the makeup of the *ERIC* database (item 52), and an additional 30.21 percent answered this item incorrectly.

A number of items, including those on the research process and searching techniques, were answered correctly by many of those surveyed. More than 60 percent understood how simple Boolean logic works (item 45), more than 50 percent knew where you would be most likely to find information about current research in education (item 47), and almost 40 percent recognized and selected the first step to begin collecting information on a topic (item 49). Almost 58 percent knew where to find related articles or books when one has identified an excellent article (item 53), and nearly 47 percent selected the "accession number" as the item least likely to help evaluate a citation (item 57).

In comparison to Morner's results on these items, without the benefit of an "I don't know" category, and given that Morner participants were all doctoral students, and some items in this section were adapted for the current sample, table 4.8 shows a side-by-side look at the results.

The last column in table 4.8 is the total percentage of individuals who answered items correctly in the current study. In almost every instance Morner's doctoral students scored higher than those in the current study. This finding is somewhat expected in that doctoral students in education fared better in this section than undergraduates and master's students. By comparison, the current study participants scores were considerably lower. This section of the survey included basic queries about education resources, topics and searching strategies. The "I don't know" category was included to eliminate guessing. This data, along with Morner study findings, confirm that common education knowledge is lacking at all levels.

Differences in the current sample between responses from undergraduates and graduates are not significant, with the largest difference being nine in item 56, "subject terms from an on-line catalog."

Table 4.8. Experience

Current Sample vs. Morner's Ph.D. Students					
Test Items	Key	Morner (percentage correct) N=149	Neely G n=54	Neely U n=74	Neely (percentage correct) N=128
43	C	59.7	19	14	25.78
44	C	40.9	2	2	03.12
45	A	71.1	43	39	64.06
46	D	43.0	16	16	25.00
47	D	87.2	38	33	55.46
48	B	28.9	11	12	17.96
49	B	44.3	22	29	39.84
50	D	31.5	12	18	23.43
51	C	24.8	5	9	10.93
52	B	53.7	15	13	21.87
53	A	89.9	36	41	60.15
54	D	08.1	3	2	03.90
55	C	61.1	11	3	10.93
56	C	30.9	9	0	07.03
57	C	63.1	29	31	46.87
58	D	67.8	24	23	36.71

Note: G—graduate students and U—undergraduate students in the Neely study.

Role of Relationship with Faculty

The relationship with faculty section was, surprisingly, the area that individuals participating in the pilot had the most problems with. Written comments included "this section could be omitted," "what does it have to do with using the library?" and "how does this section address your research questions?"[3] Previously cited professional and research literature (see Bargar and Mayo-Chamberlain 1983; Girves and Wemmerus 1988; Hockin 1981; Kammerer 1986; E. Katz 1995; J. Katz and Hartnett 1976; Lenz 1995; Lussier 1995; Manis et al. 1993; McFarland and Caplow 1995; Miller 1995; E. Rudd 1985; Winston and Polkosnik 1984; Zaporozhetz 1987) reveal and confirm the critical importance of the advisor/advisee relationship to graduate students, and the overall graduate school experience.

As noted previously, McCarthy (1985) wrote about the "faculty problem," where faculty complete research, teaching, and publishing with limited or no library use. Morner (1993) also stressed the importance of faculty encouraging students to use the library and also, to model library use behavior (p. 15). Although there is a body of student developmental research on undergraduates (Gordon 1994); research on the relationship between faculty and undergraduate students is more scarce and mostly comprised of research directed at, and surveying faculty who teach undergraduates, in an attempt to discern their attitudes about library research and the information literacy skills of their students (see Amstutz and Whitson 1997; Arp and Kenny 1990; Arp and Wilson 1989; Baxter 1990; Eichman 1979; Epp and Segal 1987; Knapp et al. 1964; Lubans 1974; Maynard 1990; Nowakowski 1993; Nowakowski and Frick 1995; Scholman et al. 1989; Stoan 1984; J. Thomas and Ensor 1982; J. Thomas 1994; Werrell and Wesley 1990).

As a function of how students acquire information literacy and library research skills and their attitudes about these skills, the student/faculty relationship is an important aspect at all levels of the academe. Although Morner (1993) discussed the quality of the relationship between the graduate student and faculty advisor, she did not include any corresponding survey items. A separate section, developed from the review of the literature section completed for the Neely (2000) research, and the findings and conclusions reported therein, was included in the Neely Test. Students (n=140) responded to seven questions about their current relationship with faculty members. In items 22, 24, 26, and 27, students were instructed to select all answers that were applicable.

In terms of faculty members encouraging the use of information in different formats (item 21), 30 percent reported that "two" faculty members had encouraged this use. A little more than 27 percent reported "three" faculty members had encouraged this use, and nearly 19 percent reported "one" faculty member engaging in this behavior. Less than 10 percent reported "none" in this section, 7.14 percent reported "four," and less than 6 percent reported "five or more."

In viewing the coursework/classroom experience with faculty members (item 22), almost 21 percent of those responding reported "faculty member(s) requires no use of outside materials for completing course requirements," and more than 50 percent reported "faculty member(s) requires use of only lectures and assigned textbook(s) for completing course assignments." These numbers are important and reveal that despite the increasing wealth of information being published and disseminated in many formats and subject areas, few professors and/or academic faculty at the Targeted University in the School of Education are taking advantage of and using the increasing technological aspects of the fast developing information movement. This can be translated to mean that fewer bodies are shouldering more of the responsibility for instructing students in library research skills and information literacy related activities.

More than 65 percent selected item 22c, "faculty member(s) requires use of library to retrieve reserve materials." This number is high and although this method is successful in getting students inside the library, does not guarantee students will stay and use additional resources. Fifty-five percent selected item 22b, "faculty member(s) requires use of only lectures and assigned textbook(s) for completing course assignments." Results for items 22d and 22e are promising and reveal that almost 56 percent selected "faculty member(s) makes use of print materials and electronic databases (on-line, CD-ROM, and/or Internet) when presenting course material and lectures"; and nearly 65 percent selected "faculty member(s) requires/suggests use of print materials and electronic databases (on-line, CD-ROM, and/or Internet) when assigning course work." The smallest percentage (20.71 percent) was recorded for item "f"—"faculty member(s) invites librarians to introduce course-related resources in print and electronic (on-line, CD-ROM, and/or Internet) formats."

These findings are somewhat comparable to Maio's (1995) dissertation findings which reported from the perspective of undergraduate faculty. Almost 74 percent require students to use information resources in addition to the textbook and lecture; more than 50 percent of the faculty used CD-ROMs and databases frequently or sometimes; and more than 45 percent reported rare or no use, or it was not applicable. Maio's intent was, among other things, to ascertain the types of resources used by faculty for themselves and to instruct their students; however, she asked no questions about reserve items.

The findings in items 22a, b, and c are consistent with published empirical research on undergraduate and graduate students which reveal that faculty expect students at all levels to possess the research and information literacy skills in order to complete assignments and research projects (see Amstutz and Whitson 1997; Dreifuss 1980; Lubans 1980; Maio 1995; Nowakowski and Frick 1995; J. Thomas and Ensor 1982; J. Thomas 1994; Zaporozhetz 1987), and in doing so, structure class assignments and coursework accordingly.

In response to whether or not students had participated in "an independent study/student initiated research with a faculty member" (item 23), 27.85 percent (39) reported that they had, and almost 70 percent had not. Of those who responded affirmatively, 22.85 percent (32) reported that "faculty had made themselves available for regular meetings providing helpful feedback and progress reports." Twenty percent (28) shared that "faculty had provided guidance and assistance in accessing resources in conducting literature reviews," 17.85 percent (25) reported "faculty was knowledgeable about deadlines and departmental guidelines," and 15.71 percent (22) selected "faculty kept me informed about matters related to my academic well being."

These items represent examples of positive, progressive interactions and relationships between faculty and students in a student initiated environment. Although the subsample is considerably smaller (perhaps a result of current study demographics), these results provide foundation data from which additional research can be conducted. Previously cited literature provides evidence which attest to the importance of this relationship and its benefits to both students and faculty (Hockin 1981); however, this study's findings from items 23 through 26, confirm previous findings from J. Katz and Hartnett (1976) that most graduate students do not have the advantage of participating in a relationship of this type with an advisor or faculty member. Findings from Hockin (1981) on the theory of the sociality/partnership relationship between advisors and Ph.D. student advisees is also confirmed here; as well as research on faculty attitudes and graduate students by E. Katz (1995), Lussier (1995), Lenz (1995), Manis et al. (1993), McFarland and Caplow (1995), and Miller (1995). The final statement in item 24 was a negative one and was selected by only 2.14 percent (3) of the subsample.

More than 20 percent (29) of those responding reported that they had participated in "directed research/teaching practicum with faculty members," item 25, and nearly 75 percent (74.28) reported that they had not. Of those answering yes, the following was reported on statements depicting a positive relationship: 14.28 percent (20)—"faculty member(s) treated me respectfully as a junior colleague"; and 12.85

percent (18)—"faculty provided constructive criticism and feedback on project/teaching effort." These findings tend to reinforce the idea that these activities are beneficial experiences for both the student and faculty.

The negative statements received substantially lower percentages from the subsample: 5.71 percent (8) reported "faculty member(s) treated me as a gopher and student help," and only 1.42 percent (2) reported "faculty did not often have time to meet with me to discuss my work." Based on the professional literature and research reported earlier, it is doubtful the numbers depicting negative relationships will decline further based on reported faculty attitudes by Kammerer (1986), McFarland and Caplow (1995), and Zaporezhetz (1987).

In terms of the relationships that have been experienced by students reported in items 23 and 25, item 27 asked how these relationships began. Of those indicating they had participated in the types of relationships described, 15.71 percent (22) each indicated that the relationship had begun because the "faculty member was highly regarded in the subject area of interest," and that the "faculty member was recommended/assigned by the department." A little over 14 percent (20) each reported that they had "had a prior relationship with the faculty member," and that the "faculty member invited them to participate in the research project/teaching course." Ten percent (14) reported that the "faculty member was recommended by other students/faculty."

Summary

This section presented the findings from the exposure, experience, and research with faculty sections. The exposure section queried respondents on their exposure to the library environment currently, in the academic program they were enrolled in at the time of the survey, and in general, their entire academic careers. Findings were compatible with those of previously reported research that students at all academic levels, overwhelmingly, are not being exposed to the library research environment. Significant numbers were reported in the "0 times" column and the numbers generally decreased across the board as the amount of time exposed increased (see tables 4.5 and 4.6). When undergraduates in the sample were compared to graduate students, the latter appeared to have more exposure than the former, although this may be a result of being enrolled in an academic program for a longer period of time (i.e., graduate school vs. undergraduate school). Toomer's (1993) assertions for adult learners were further confirmed by the current study findings for self-learning methodologies.

Formal library instruction at the minimal level was considered helpful, and findings on when participants first learned to use the library confirmed previously reported research by Alire (1984), Damko (1991), and Simon (1995), that the most frequently reported ways of learning to use the library were self-teaching and high school. An interesting find is that more than 18 percent of the current sample learned to use the library in elementary or grade school, and an additional 4 respondents were taught by their parents.

All items in the experience section were adapted from the Morner Test of Library Research Skills. This section is the only one in the Neely Test with one correct answer for each item. The inclusion of the "I don't know" option appears to have decreased the tendency to guess (see table 4.7). This assumption is based on the significant total percentages reported in the "I don't know" column. Responses reveal the majority of those surveyed understood Boolean logic, identified the first step in the beginning of the research process, and knew how to locate additional relevant materials when given an excellent article on a topic.

These findings are consistent with previously reported research on graduate and undergraduate students which noted the inadequate knowledge of subject area resources for both groups. In comparing Morner's doctoral students with the current study participants, it is revealed that doctoral students answered more items correctly than those responding in the current study.

The relationship with faculty section is the section that members of the survey pilot had the most difficulty in terms of understanding why it was included. Professional and research literature presented previously attest to the importance of the faculty/student relationship at all academic levels in all areas.

Findings for this area reveal that few students are being influenced by faculty members in terms of information literacy and library research skills. Of those reporting the nature of the coursework/classroom experience, nearly three-fourths each reported "faculty member(s) requires no use of outside materials for completing course requirements," and "faculty member(s) requires use of only lectures and assigned textbooks(s) for completing course assignments." A large portion of the sample reported that "faculty member(s) requires use of library to retrieve reserve materials," but this only guarantees students will come into the library and then, once inside, only go as far as the loan/reserve desk. With the increased trends in electronic reserves, the need for these students to actually step into a library may decline.

Few students reported being involved in direct relationships (independent study/directed research/teaching practicums) and, of those, the relationships were overall positive. The majority of these relationships developed because the "faculty member had been recommended or assigned by the department," or "was highly regarded in the subject area of interest."

The next section presents findings for the predicting relevance section. This section will disseminate data gathered on attitudes about information literacy skills and performance on evaluative queries.

Predicting Relevance

This section will present and discuss descriptive statistics on students' attitudes about information literacy skills and the results of the performance section where students were queried about their perceptions when evaluating information. It will also address research questions 3 and 4: (3) What are the attitudes and perceptions of college-level students about Doyle's (1992) ten information literacy skills?; and (4) What are the attitudes and perceptions of college-level students about pre-identified relevance evaluative criteria?

Role of Attitude

To date, H. Morrison's (1997) attitudinal research on information literacy skills is the sole published empirical evidence of how students feel about these skills. Unfortunately, H. Morrison's focus group only responded to what was identified as the four main information literacy skills—recognizing a need for information, locating information, evaluating information, and effectively using information—loosely corresponding to items 11, 16, 17, and 20 in the current study. The Neely Test included a section on attitudes about information literacy skills and the findings are presented in tables 4.9 and 4.10.

The data collected in this section greatly increases the scarce empirical literature on students' attitudes about information literacy skills, while providing solid evidence on which to base further discussions and empirical investigations. It also adds significantly to the body of prescriptive professional literature which typically has not included the students' point of view (see Bruce 1997, pp. 75-76). Many of the skills, specifically "evaluating information," are also investigated further in the performance section.

For the first two skills, students were asked to indicate their levels of agreement and disagreement by responding to Likert type queries, and for the remaining eight skills, students were asked to indicate their comfort level. Very few students (three) responding to this section strongly disagreed or reported being very uncomfortable when faced with the skills, as shown in the last columns of tables 4.9 and 4.10.

Table 4.9. Attitude

Attitudes about information literacy skills—1					
	Percentages Responding				
N=139	SA	A	U/N	D	SD
Recognize that accurate and complete information . . .	56.11	41.00	01.43	0.00	0
When faced with a problem . . .	24.46	58.99	10.07	5.03	0

Note: SA—strongly agree, A—agree, U/N—undecided/neutral, D—disagree, SD—strongly disagree.

Skills 1 and 2

More than 55 percent (78) strongly agreed and 41 percent (57) agreed that they "recognized accurate and complete information as the basis of intelligent decision making." Nearly 60 percent (83) agreed that "when faced with a problem in daily life, they generally try to find information as the first step in solving the problem," and almost one quarter (34) strongly agreed. This item was worded in the survey instrument as "recognizes the need for information." A little more than 10 percent (14) were undecided/neutral about this skill and more than 5 percent (7) disagreed.

H. Morrison's (1997) findings on this skill revealed that there was "disagreement about whether or not recognizing a need for information constitutes a 'skill'" (p. 7). There is little room for comparison of the current results to H. Morrison's study because unlike the focus group methodology, the quantitative nature of the current study did not allow for commentary on this question. It could be argued, perhaps, that disagreement with a skill implies that it is not recognized as a skill; however, this study, based on the research literature reported earlier (Doyle 1992), presumes that all ten are skills and this was not the purpose of this section of the current study. Table 4.9 also reveals that no participant disagreed or strongly disagreed with this skill.

Table 4.10. Attitude

Attitudes about information literacy skills—2					
	Percentages Responding				
N=139	VC	C	U/N	U	VU
Formulates questions based on info. needs	24.46	53.23	17.98	02.87	0.000
Identifies potential sources of information	20.14	59.71	10.79	07.91	0.000
Develops successful search strategies	14.38	43.16	25.17	14.38	0.719
Accesses sources of information . . .	15.82	44.60	20.14	16.54	1.430
Evaluates information	23.74	55.39	16.54	02.87	0.000
Organizes information for practical application	28.05	54.67	10.07	05.75	0.000
Integrates new information . . .	21.58	58.99	12.23	05.75	0.000
Uses information in critical thinking . . .	32.37	54.67	06.47	02.87	0.000

Note: VC—very comfortable, C—comfortable, U/N—undecided/neutral, U—uncomfortable, V/U—very uncomfortable.

Skills 3 through 10

More than 50 percent (74) of the respondents reported feeling comfortable "formulating questions based on information needs," and nearly a quarter (34) reported feeling very comfortable. Less than 18 percent (25) reported feeling undecided/neutral with this skill.

Almost 60 percent (80) of those responding reported that they felt comfortable "identifying potential sources of information," and more than 20 percent (28) reported they felt very uncomfortable.

More than 55 percent (80) reported that they felt either very comfortable or comfortable "developing successful search strategies," and more than a quarter (35) reported feeling undecided/neutral about the skill.

"Accessing sources of information including computer-based and other technologies" is the sixth of Doyle's (1992) information literacy skills, Neely Test item 16. Nearly 45 percent (62) of those responding to this item reported feeling comfortable, and almost 16 percent (22) reported feeling very comfortable with this skill. More than 20 percent (28) reported feeling undecided/neutral, and nearly 17 percent (23) reported feeling uncomfortable. This skill loosely corresponds to H. Morrison's "locating information," skill.

"Evaluating information" is the skill upon which this study is primarily based in that it presupposes that the ability to evaluate information is the most critical information literacy skill. The role of performance section is a companion to this skill in that all of the items depict evaluating information. Less than one fourth of the sample (23.74 percent) reported feeling very comfortable, and 55.39 percent reported being comfortable with this skill. Almost 17 percent (23) reported feeling undecided/neutral and four persons reported feeling uncomfortable. H. Morrison's findings on this skill revealed that the undergraduates were unanimous in agreeing that evaluating information was the most advanced skill of the four. H. Morrison also reported that the students felt less than confident in their ability to evaluate information (p. 7). Her findings do not appear to be in line with the self-reported findings of this section of the study. Further analysis will be conducted in the performance section.

In terms of "organizing information for practical application," a large portion of the sample (115) reported feeling either very comfortable or comfortable with this skill, and a majority of the sample (112) responded that they felt very comfortable or comfortable "integrating new information into an existing body of knowledge."

Almost 55 percent (76) reported feeling comfortable "using information in critical thinking and problem solving," and nearly 33 percent

(45) reported feeling very comfortable. H. Morrison's query on this skill was worded slightly different and, thus, her students responded to how they felt about "effectively using information." The focus group discussed such issues as formatting, plagiarizing, creating an original work, and the impact of the information on the reader (p. 7). This skill will be further explored in the performance section as well.

Role of Performance

All of the items in this section were developed to find out the students' knowledge and perceptions on queries depicting evaluating information, and also, the effectiveness of those evaluative judgments made based on the students knowledge and perceptions. This was the longest section of the survey instrument, designed to include many possible aspects of the process of evaluating information. Some of the items were adapted from the Morner Test, and others were developed based on the review of the literature and published research. It should also be noted that the items to which the participants were responding represented the myriad of possibilities one is faced with when conducting research in proprietary databases, which sometimes contain abstracts and/or indexes, and sometimes only bibliographic citations.

Item 28 was developed to find out students' perceptions of what type of information is most or least useful in doing research, on a scale of five to one with the former being most useful. Item 29 was developed to find out about criteria used to select an article for a research project using a scale of five (include) to one (exclude). Tables 4.11 and 4.12 show findings for these items.

Table 4.11. Performance

Most (5) and least (1) useful criteria

Percentages Responding

	Most useful			Least useful	
Criteria	5	4	3	2	1
a. available in a research library	51.79	26.61	15.82	00.719	01.430
b. indexed in a computer database	42.44	28.77	18.70	05.750	00.719
c. published in a refereed journal	21.58	28.77	33.81	10.790	01.430
d. written by university faculty	10.07	26.61	35.97	17.980	05.750
e. published in a textbook	21.58	36.69	25.17	10.070	02.870
f. thesis and dissertations	05.75	19.42	41.72	17.980	10.790

Table 4.12. Performance

Most likely to Include (5) or Exclude (1)

Percentages Responding

		Include			Exclude	
	Criteria	5	4	3	2	1
a.	article available only by interlibrary loan/ not available locally	10.07	13.66	20.14	30.93	21.58
b.	full text of article not available locally	12.23	26.61	32.37	17.98	06.47
c.	article too long	03.59	17.98	43.16	24.46	07.19
d.	abstract not included with citation	05.03	12.94	34.53	27.33	16.54
e.	article is too advanced/ technical	02.15	10.79	32.37	25.89	25.17
f.	article is too general	02.87	07.19	32.37	36.69	16.54

Items 28 and 29 were adapted from the Morner Test (Morner items 22 and 30) and supplemented by the author's reading of the published research literature on relevance. When the findings of the current study are compared with Morner's, it is revealed that doctoral students over-whelmingly believe refereed journals have the most scholarly, re-spected research. In contrast, more than half the respondents in the cur-rent study (72) believe an item is most useful if it is "available in a research library." The next highly rated criteria was "indexed in a com-puter database," selected by fifty-nine participants. "Published in a refereed journal" and "published in a textbook" each were selected by thirty of the respondents, ranking third in the most useful (5) category.

"Theses and dissertations" was selected by fifty-eight individuals with a neutral score of "3," as was "written by university faculty," which was selected by fifty individuals, and "published in a refereed journal," selected by forty-seven participants. Fifteen of the respondents believed that "theses and dissertations" are the least useful in doing research. Of those fifteen, five were master's students and four were seniors. Twenty-five respondents gave the same category a score of "2," the majority of whom were undergraduate seniors and master's students. It is interesting to find that twenty-one master' students (41.17 percent), and 100 percent of the doctoral students in the sample are neutral about the usefulness of "theses and dissertations," as the demonstrated ability to produce original research is a major and critical part in many, if not most terminal degree programs.

Table 4.12 presents the findings for those items most likely to be included (5) or excluded (1) when selecting articles for a research project. Only fourteen of those responding would be most likely to include an article if it was "available only via interlibrary loan." Half of those were master's students and one was a doctoral student. In contrast, thirty individuals reported that an article in the same category was least likely to be included. These findings on interlibrary loan echo and confirm research reported by Farid et. al. (1984) which found that 6.2 percent of those taking coursework and 13.5 percent of those at the dissertation stage reported not using interlibrary loan services at all. This finding is discouraging in that no one academic library in the current age of decreasing budgets and increasing serial prices and inflation can subscribe to every serial subscription. Interlibrary loan and document delivery services provide access to the wealth of information beyond local library holdings. It should not be considered a negative criteria. It should also be noted that items in table 4.12 represent, to some degree, how and why students make relevance judgments. This item will be further explored in the relevance section.

Table 4.12 reveals significantly more higher numbers in the "2" column (close to exclude) than in the "4" column (close to include) for five of the six categories. It should be noted that in responding to this item, students were considering the selection of articles, and the articles being selected were most likely, for a wide range of projects at each of the academic levels. These findings should not be interpreted without considering the wide array of possibilities for the final project (three to five page freshman composition paper with five references; a master's thesis).

A number of items with significant numbers received a somewhat neutral or indifferent score of "3." Sixty respondents were indifferent bout an "article that is too long," forty-eight an article where the "abstract is not included with citation," and forty-five each about an article that the "full text is not available electronically," "article is too advanced/technical," and where the "article is too general." In interpreting the number of individuals who gave scores of "3," one should consider that indifference does not necessarily denote negativity; it could also be construed as the person does not have an opinion or maybe has not been exposed to a particular situation. Unfortunately the academic status distribution does not appear to reveal any significant patterns in the neutral categories, with the exception of master's students, who comprise a large part of the sample, weighing heavily in most areas. (See table A.2, appendix A.)

The academic distribution for those with scores of "5" (most useful/likely to include) is a bit more illuminating as shown in table A.3, appendix A. The total number for many categories is extremely low. As stated previously, it is not likely, nor is it realistic to expect that a local library will own all of the resources one needs on a particular topic, nor that databases which are 100 percent full text will be the answer to most research dilemmas. The criteria represented in these items should not be interpreted as negative, nor as a barrier to information access. Given that the researcher has allocated the appropriate amount of time in conducting a thorough literature review, and that interlibrary loan is a viable option, the majority or all of the items needed can be acquired and reviewed for use in research projects (see table 4.12). In contrast, the significant number of seniors, master's, and doctoral students who felt that items "available in a research library" and "indexed in a computer database" are more useful, is of concern (see table 4.11). As are the marked small numbers for "theses and dissertations" with a score of "5." Students in the current study felt that these items ("available in a research library" and "indexed in a computer database") were more useful to them in their research than the other categories listed including "published in a refereed journal," "theses and dissertations," or "written by university faculty." A common misconception among library users in the current technological age is that "everything" is on the computer. Findings from the current study confirm this is still a problem. All researchers, students, or otherwise must be aware of the exponential volume of information and data that is available and also, must possess the skills necessary to evaluate and make accurate relevance judgments about all types of information in all formats.

In the determination of whether or not research is complete, item 30, respondents were able to select more than one answer. Morner's (1993) results for a similar item found that 66 percent of doctoral students recognized their research as being complete when "new bibliographies yield familiar citations." Findings from the current study reveal that 88.48 percent of the sample believed their research was complete if "information in secondary and tertiary sources is confirmed by information found in primary sources," and when "citations in published bibliographies, including those located at the end of books and articles are largely similar." Unfortunately, only 27.33 percent of those selected the latter response.

Nearly 70 percent believed their research was complete when "all resources suggested by professors, librarians, and/or teaching assistants [had] been examined." More disconcerting and a testament to the pro-liferation of electronic databases, the Internet, and commonly believed misconceptions that "everything is on the computer," is the nearly 63 percent who believed their research was complete when "all subject-related on-line and electronic databases [had] been searched," and the 49.64 percent who believed their research was complete when "all rele-vant materials (books and articles) owned by the local library [had] been examined." The latter two are consistent with the significant num-ber of participants, nearly one half the sample, who felt that "availabil-ity in a research library" (43.88 percent) and "indexed in a computer database" (42.44 percent) were criteria most likely to be used, and most useful in doing research and selecting articles for a research project.

Table A.4, appendix A, shows the detailed findings for item 31, perception of reliable resources. The responses are promising in that all queries are positive statements, and each one was selected by at least 50 percent of the sample, with two statements being selected by more than 80 percent. Findings for statements in item 32, when one would use "an article located on the Internet" in a research project, are promising as well, with the exception of the 64 percent who would use an article in a research project simply because the "full text was available." It should also be noted that more than 50 percent of the sample would use an article written by "an individual with a Ph.D." from the Internet, yet, the dissertation, a major part of obtaining a Ph.D., is not seen as an im-portant resource in and of itself, as reported previously in disseminating data from items 28 and 29 (see table 11). Complete results for items 31 and 32 can be found in table A.4, Appendix A.

The Neely Test was administered in November and December of 1998, near the end of the semester, and in January and February of 1999. Considering half the sample data was collected during the fall 1998 semester, findings for item 33, "how many times respondents have accessed on-line databases (including the catalog) for information for problem-solving" are not as high as was expected, given the time frame being late in the semester. Only 38.12 percent of the sample re-ported having accessed databases "7 or more times." Nearly 18 percent have accessed databases "5-6 times," less than 17 percent "1-2 times," and less than 15 percent "3-4 times." Less than 12 percent have ac-cessed databases "0 times."

Item 34 was developed to ask students about the types of information formats they use to solve information problems. "Accessing sources of information including computer-based and other technologies" is an information literacy skill (Doyle [1992] skill 6) and this question lists many such formats of information. Occasional use in all categories is mostly in the twentieth to thirtieth percentile (see table 4.13). For commonly used sources like the "on-line catalog," on-line and print "indexes and abstracts," "statistical sources," and "government documents," the findings are disheartening. Nearly a quarter of the sample use "on-line catalogs" infrequently or never, and the use of print and on-line "indexes and abstracts" is even more revealing, with 41 percent using printed ones infrequently or never, and 32.37 percent reporting infrequent or no use of on-line versions. "Government documents" comprise a large part of education resources considering the publication output of the U.S. Department of Education, however, nearly 50 percent admitted to infrequent or no use of these resources. With the exception of journal and magazine articles and monographs indexed in *ERIC*, resources from this database are usually received in libraries on microfiche. Almost 65 percent of the sample reported using "microfilm/fiche" either infrequently or never.

Forty-one percent use "Internet tools," which include the World Wide Web, telnet and ftp (file transfer protocol), very frequently, and 28.77 percent reported frequent use. In comparison with previously reported research, these findings are in contrast with those reported by Farid et al. (1984) who reported that the most frequently used resource among Ph.D. students was the on-line catalog. It should be noted that the current user interface for the researcher's home university's on-line catalog, in addition to the ASCII version, is via Netscape™,[4] or some other Internet browser. Survey construction and subsequent findings do not allow for a clear distinction between the catalog and other Internet tools in this instance, however, table 4.13 reveals that current study participants use journals and magazines more frequently than any other resource.

Ten percent more students (53 percent) in the Farid et al. (1984) study reported using abstracts and indexes frequently than in the current study, but 32.36 percent in the current study never use these types of resources, compared to the almost 20 percent (18.98 percent) in the Farid et al. study. More than 50 percent of the current sample reported using "journals and magazines" frequently or very frequently. It is not possible to discern whether or not the sample recognized the difference between the categories of "journals and magazines," and "indexes and abstracts," in that one is generally used to access the contents of the other. Table 4.13 shows the complete findings for item 34.

Item 35 is concerned with the students' knowledge about searching techniques. In line with the considerable number of "I don't know" (36.69 percent) and incorrect (34.52 percent) responses to the "truncation" item (#46) in the experience section (see table 4.7), only 10.79 percent reported using "truncation" in searching either frequently, or very frequently, and nearly 70 percent reported using it either infrequently or never. The Boolean operator "or" is used occasionally by nearly 30 percent of the sample, and operators "and" and "not" are used occasionally by almost 26 percent. "Limiters" are used frequently or very frequently by more than 45 percent, and occasionally by nearly a quarter of the sample. "Proximity" searching is rarely done with almost 80 percent reporting either infrequent or no usage.

Findings from the experience section item on selecting subject headings for an on-line catalog (#56) where more than 46 percent "did not know," and 35.96 percent answered incorrectly, are consistent with the current section where almost 55 percent infrequently or never use "descriptors" or "some other controlled vocabulary." These findings are clearly in contrast with the self-reported attitudes about "developing successful search strategies" reported previously, where more than half of the sample (57.55 percent) reported feeling very comfortable or comfortable with this skill. Students who report they were comfortable with developing successful strategies are apparently not making use of the many search strategy options available on various on-line sources. It could be concluded that these students are simply not aware of their inadequate search strategy knowledge. Table 4.14 shows the complete findings for this item.

Item 36 was included because it illuminates the information literacy skills process, specifically (Doyle 1992) skills 8 and 9 (organizes information for practical application, and integrates new information into an existing body of knowledge). It appears that in this self-report section, a majority of the steps are reportedly done either very frequently or frequently, and occasional use is reported for all except three in the twentieth to thirtieth percentile within the sample. These findings raise interesting questions, however, they are self-reported findings and should be interpreted as such. A more detailed discussion of the nature of self-report data can be found in the summary for this section. Complete data for this item is revealed in table 4.15.

Table 4.13. Current use of information in various formats

		VF %	VF #	F %	F #	O %	O #	I %	I #	N %	N #
a.	On-line catalog-books	18.70	26	23.02	32	31.65	44	13.66	19	09.35	13
b.	Journals/magazines	28.77	40	23.02	46	22.30	31	08.63	12	03.59	5
c.	Subject encyclopedias	05.03	7	33.09	15	29.49	41	27.33	38	23.74	33
d.	Subject dictionaries	03.59	5	10.79	9	22.30	31	31.65	44	30.93	43
e.	Biographical sources	04.31	6	06.47	20	26.61	37	25.89	36	24.46	34
f.	Research guides	07.19	10	14.38	21	30.93	43	24.46	34	17.98	25
g.	Bibliographies	07.19	10	15.10	21	26.61	37	28.77	40	18.70	26
h.	Indexes and abstracts—print	07.19	10	16.54	23	30.93	43	21.58	30	19.42	27
i.	Indexes and abstracts—on-line	12.23	17	26.61	37	25.17	35	19.42	27	12.94	18
j.	Statistical sources	05.75	8	15.10	21	23.74	33	23.74	33	26.61	37
k.	Handbooks	3.59	5	11.51	16	29.49	41	24.46	34	27.33	38
l.	Government docs.	5.03	7	11.51	16	30.21	42	23.74	33	25.17	35
m.	Internet tools	41	57	28.77	40	14.38	20	05.03	7	06.47	9
n.	Microfilm/fiche	3.59	5	07.19	10	20.14	28	25.89	36	38.84	54

Note: VF—very frequently, F—frequently, O—occasionally, I—infrequently, N—never

Table 4.14. Use of searching techniques among sample

		VF		F		O		I		N	
		%	#	%	#	%	#	%	#	%	#
a.	Truncation	02.87	4	07.91	11	17.98	25	20.86	29	47.48	66
b.	Boolean operator "or"	08.63	12	15.10	21	28.77	40	22.30	31	22.30	31
c.	Boolean operators "and" and "not"	15.82	22	23.74	33	25.89	36	15.10	21	15.10	21
d.	Limiters	14.38	20	31.65	44	24.46	34	14.38	20	12.23	17
e.	Proximity operators	00.00	0	01.43	2	15.82	22	31.65	44	46.76	65
f.	Cross and multiple field searching	12.94	18	17.98	25	34.53	48	15.82	22	15.10	21
g.	Use of descriptors and controlled vocabulary	10.07	14	11.51	16	20.86	29	15.82	22	38.84	54

Note: VF—very frequently, F—frequently, O—occasionally, I—infrequently, N—never

Table 4.15. Steps in Information Literacy skills 8 and 9

		VF		F		O		I		N	
		%	#	%	#	%	#	%	#	%	#
a.	Understand all the information	08.63	12	56.11	78	25.17	35	05.75	8	1.430	2
b.	Discuss findings with friends and colleagues	15.10	21	33.81	47	33.81	47	12.23	17	2.150	3
c.	Sort your materials by similarity of content	23.02	32	51.07	71	18.70	26	03.59	5	0.719	1
d.	Divide information by concepts and terms into topical outline	17.26	24	34.53	48	25.89	36	14.38	20	5.030	7
e.	Review the original research questions	24.46	34	48.92	68	15.82	22	07.19	10	0.000	0
f.	Discard irrelevant or useless information	33.09	46	45.32	63	12.23	17	04.31	6	1.430	2
g.	Reorganize information into topical outline	17.98	25	34.53	48	30.21	42	09.35	13	4.310	6
h.	Compare outline to research questions and adjust for modification	14.38	20	35.97	50	29.49	41	10.79	15	5.750	8
i.	Examine outline for more logical reorganization	12.94	18	41.00	57	25.89	36	12.94	18	4.310	6
j.	Look at materials under each outline heading and synthesize major points and concepts	20.86	29	43.16	60	20.14	28	07.91	11	4.310	6

Note: VF—very frequently, F—frequently, O—occasionally, I—infrequently, N—never

Item 37 is similar to item 36, however, it contains a particular subject and asks the student to number the given statements in the order of importance they would be followed in the research process. Ten individuals each reported they would first "browse a current printed magazine index," and "browse the most recent issue of an education journal." Surprisingly, twenty-four individuals reported they would first "search the Internet using keywords 'violence' and 'high schools.'" Seventy-seven reported they would first "brainstorm the concept, using the terms in the topic," and twenty-one reported they would first "formulate questions based on the information needed to begin the research."

Eighteen persons reported they would "search *ERIC* and other related databases" last, and twenty-six reported they would never include this as a step in the research process. Twenty-one would "browse a current printed magazine index" last, and twenty-five would never include this as a step.

In general, these findings are not good. It appears that respondents are more meticulous and methodical in the steps outlined in item 36 which take place *after* data has been gathered, than in the actual gathering of the data itself. The results suggest that the research process itself is unfamiliar or simply unlearned given the earlier findings of this study, that almost 58 percent first learned to use the library on their own or in high school; an additional 18.57 percent first learned in elementary or grade school. Findings for item 37 are also in direct contrast with the self-reported attitude section where nearly 80 percent reported feeling very comfortable or comfortable "identifying potential sources of information;" more than 60 percent felt very comfortable or comfortable accessing sources of information including computer-based and other technologies; and 57.54 percent reported being very comfortable or comfortable developing successful search strategies (see table 4.10). Other findings for this item are shown in table 4.16.

The final steps in the information literacy process are depicted in item 38. Respondents were instructed to select all answers that were applicable to them. "When writing up information found for a research project or presentation," almost 75 percent each reported they would "write/present based on a combination of reflection and opinions (theirs, author(s)), and previously read material," and "reflect on what they had read and formulate and present their own opinion." Nearly 70 percent would "write/present based on a combination of reflection and opinions (theirs and author(s));" and more than 55 percent reported they would "write/present what they believe the author(s) said."

Table 4.16. Steps in the research process with a known topic

"Violence in American high schools"	Never	1st	2nd	3rd	4th	5th	6th	7th
1. Browse a current printed magazine index	25	10	8	10	18	19	21	21
2. Browse the most recent issue of an education journal	17	10	12	8	19	29	27	11
3. Search the Internet using keywords "violence" and "high schools"	2	24	10	36	28	17	12	4
4. Look at reference material that provides an overview of violence and teenagers	5	9	10	38	26	26	15	4
5. Brainstorm the concept, using the terms in the topic	13	77	23	4	5	2	7	2
6. Formulate questions based on the information needed to begin the research	19	21	62	8	9	4	2	7
7. Search *ERIC* and other related databases	26	11	11	24	18	15	11	18

Smaller numbers were reported, more than 28 percent each, by those who would "write/present what they thought the instructor or professor wanted to hear," and "write/present the opinions of the author verbatim," the latter of which is a phenomena commonly known as plagiarizing. Of those selecting these categories, the academic status is as follows: 38c. "write/present what they thought the instructor or professor wanted to hear"—three freshmen; two sophomores; five juniors; ten seniors; fourteen master's; four other; and one individual who did not indicate academic status. 38d. "write/present the opinions of the author verbatim"—one freshman; five sophomores; two juniors; eleven seniors; seventeen master's; one Ph.D. student; one other; and two individuals who did not indicate academic status. Only 6.47 percent would "write/present their opinions only."

These findings further illuminate the unreliable nature of self-reported data. Previously (see table 4.10), more than 80 percent of the sample reported they felt comfortable or very comfortable "integrating new information into an existing body of knowledge," and more than 87 percent reported feeling very comfortable or comfortable when "using information in critical thinking and problem solving." When viewed in conjunction with additional quantitative data from item 38, it is clear that participants' confidence/comfort levels about their skills appear to be exaggerated.

Summary and Discussion

This section presented the results of the predicting relevance section. Responses to the evaluative questions in the performance section provide information that may be used to predict the effectiveness of evaluative judgments.

The limited comparison of the current section findings with previously reported research can be attributed to the limited empirical evidence on information literacy skills as a whole, and evaluation skills in particular. The researcher was unable to find comparable or similar items represented empirically or professionally in the literature. Thus, the evidence presented here provides data upon which a substantive discussion of students' evaluation skills can be based and also as comparison for further empirical exploration.

Greer, Weston, and Alm's 1991 survey of library users (n=694) "examined the validity of self-assessment of library skills by measuring objectively determined skill levels" (p. 550). There were 559 undergraduates in the survey. The researchers found that "self-assessment was an unreliable method for judging students' research capabilities" (pp. 552-53). Self-reported findings in the current study on attitudes about information literacy skills, particularly, the skill of evaluation, are clearly in contrast with findings in the performance section, as well as findings from H. Morrison (1997) who reported that undergraduate students' surveyed were less than confident about their ability to evaluate information, listing credibility as a primary concern (p. 7).

In reviewing specific items previously discussed in the performance section, in direct contrast to the self-reported comfort levels of the current section, more than 50 percent of the sample reported that they believed an item "available in a research library" was most useful in doing research, 42.44 percent reported they believed items "indexed in a computer database" are most useful, and 41 percent reported being neutral about the usefulness of "theses and dissertations" (see table 4.11). On-line and print indexes and abstracts, microfilm/fiche, government documents, and statistical sources are not used very frequently or frequently by many of the students (see table 4.16). More than half of the sample (52.51 percent) reported that they would not include an item when selecting articles for a research project if it were "only available by interlibrary loan," and significant numbers were reported for the neutral category of "3" for items where the "full text was not available electronically" (32.37 percent), the "article was too long" (43.16 percent), the "article was too general"(32.37 percent), and where an "abstract was not included with the citation" (34.53 percent) (see table A.4, appendix A). These findings present a clear contrast between individuals selecting these items and the nearly 80 percent who previously reported feeling very comfortable or comfortable identifying potential sources of information.

Evaluative criteria for reliable resources revealed many of the respondents (67.62 percent) consider an item reliable if it is found on the "Internet or in on-line databases," and more than 50 percent consider those items "used by other students and colleagues" reliable (see table A.4). These findings appear to be in direct contrast with the nearly 80 percent of the sample who reported being comfortable or very comfortable evaluating information.

Nearly 99 percent of the sample agreed or strongly agreed that they recognized that accurate and complete information is the basis for intelligent decision making; however, less than 30 percent of those responding recognized when their information was complete.

In terms of comfort levels reported in developing successful search strategies, nearly 60 percent reported being very comfortable or comfortable with this skill. However, in viewing findings from items on the use of searching techniques, large percentages of the sample reported infrequent or no use of descriptors and controlled vocabulary (54.66

percent), proximity operators (78.41 percent), or truncation (68.34 percent).

In general, findings for the performance section were in contrast, sometimes directly, with self-reported attitude comfort levels about information literacy skills, and should be viewed and interpreted in conjunction with other detailed relevant survey data.

Research Question 3: What are the attitudes and perceptions of college-level students about Doyle's (1992) ten information literacy skills?

Discussion: Overall, the data (see tables 4.9 and 4.10) reveals that the majority of the sample either strongly agreed or agreed, or reported being very comfortable or comfortable with the ten information literacy skills. Viewed in conjunction with additional data gathered for items in the performance section, the positive attitudes appear to be greatly exaggerated and perhaps misguided. These findings clearly confirm the unreliable nature of self-report data alone and, as well, the importance of including related survey items which depict, in this case, the attitudinal items (see Greer et al. 1991). These findings also point out the dichotomous nature of the students' perceived comfort levels and their actual performance, thus, confirming a clear need for information literacy and instructional skills intervention for all education students at the Targeted University.

Relevance

As reported earlier in this study, there have only been three studies which solicit and report on user-based relevance criteria in information science (see Barry 1991; T. K. Park 1992; Schamber 1991), and the closest terminology to relevance in the library science literature is evaluation. Survey items 39 through 42 were constructed from the findings of the previously mentioned three dissertations which reported on data taken directly from individuals on relevance judgments made when deciding whether or not to use information and/or citations.

Respondents in the current study were asked to report their comfort levels, using a Likert type scale, for 27 previously identified relevance criteria. The following discussion includes categories developed by Barry (1993), T. K. Park (1992), and Schamber (1991), based on user-based relevance criteria, and current study data of attitudes to provide a solid basis, grounded empirically, on the critical importance of user-based relevance criteria. This discussion will contribute to the library science evaluation and information science relevance literature and provide wider exposure, and a marrying of the information and library science relevance/evaluation dichotomy that had not been attempted prior to this study.

Schamber's 1991 dissertation (n=18) was an exploratory study which "focused on describing users' criteria for evaluation in multimedia information seeking and use situations. . . . The criteria were considered to be dimensions of relevance' (p. 1).

T. K. Park's 1992 dissertation (n=10) was exploratory in nature and sought to learn how end users evaluate citations "produced in a document retrieval system as a result of the research for an answer to his/her information problem" (p. 42). She identified a "model of a user's interpretation of relevance . . . based on the thought processes while evaluating a bibliographic citation produced by a document retrieval system" (p. 143). T. K. Park's categories in her model of relevance include the following:

> *Internal context* presents those inner levels of sources which are linked to the citation level . . . are related to an individual's perceptions and assumptions held in the problem area: the individual's previous experience with and perceptions of an author, academic programs, journals, and his or her own belief of the information problem reflects the user's conceptual state of knowledge or image of the world. An individual's level of expertise in the subject literature and previous research experience can be regarded as his private knowledge structure. (pp. 146-47)

> *External context* represents contexts where the individual's research and search for information are situated. The category of external context constitutes an individual's information seeking context and provides an explanation as to how the context is influenced by an individual's particular need situations and perceptions about information searches. The user's perception about the search in terms of search quality, search goal, and availability of information seems to affect his selection behavior in general. (p. 147)

> *Problem context* category illustrates why and how the user uses information in the process of constructing and solving his or her information problem. . . . Users are constantly seeking leads, ideas, and issues in order to understand the information problem at hand. Users are relying on the citation not only in the direct problem area but also in the different disciplines to expand their ideas—ways of thinking about what they do. As a result, the problem is reformulated and reshaped in terms of bringing new insights into their own problem area and changing their thoughts on approach and methodology. (p. 149)

The intent of Barry's 1993 dissertation (n=39) was to "explore and describe the full range of criteria that affect judgments of relevance by users evaluating printed, textual material" (p. 57). She developed coding schemes for traits and qualities to categorize and identify the information found in the responses/raw interview data. "The primary difference between traits and qualities was the extent to which they were inherent to the document and could be determined by someone other than the actual user" (p. 79).

> *Traits* were defined as tangible characteristics of documents mentioned by respondents (for example, the length of the document or the author of the document); *qualities* were defined as more subjective judgments of documents (for example, the degree to which the respondent agreed or disagreed with statements presented within the document) or situational factors (for example, the time constraints under which the respondent was working). (p. 73)

Criteria resulting from these three dissertations were separated into four categories—characteristics about: when research is conducted; the article; what is in the article; and where the article came from. As in the experience section, an "I don't know" column was added to each item in this section. Complete findings are disseminated in table 4.17 and a complete discussion of the current study findings along with the supporting definitions of criteria from the above referenced research follows.

Table 4.17. Relevance: Levels of importance for relevance judgment criteria

	VI	I	NI	DK
When research is conducted:				
1. Previous experience (P)	64	67	4	2
2. Perceptions about the author (P)	8	69	56	4
3. Perceptions about journals (P)	19	81	31	6
4. Perceptions about search quality (P)	37	82	13	4
5. Priority of information needs (P)	63	67	5	1
6. Quality vs. quantity (P)	67	57	10	3
7. Where you are in search process (P)	28	81	21	7
8. End product (P)	79	56	1	1
9. Perception of information available on chosen topic (P)	41	86	7	2
10. Time constraints (B)	66	62	4	3
11. Relationship with author (B)	5	15	81	33
Characteristics about article:				
12. Title (P)	37	62	34	1
13. Style of title (P)	9	31	89	5
14. Status of author (P)	14	72	37	10
15. Quality of publication (journal) (P)	59	62	10	3
What is in the article:				
16. Accuracy (S)	113	23	0	0
17. Currency (S)	82	49	2	2
18. Specificity (S)	63	62	4	4
19. Geographic proximity of subject (S)	18	64	44	10
20. Verifiability (S)	65	56	9	3
21. Clarity (S)	84	50	1	0
22. Information provided was new (P)	45	66	20	3
Where article came from:				
23. Accessibility (S)	80	54	2	1
24. Reliability (S)	92	42	1	1
25. Source novelty (B)	26	58	38	15
26. Document novelty (B)	28	59	35	15
27. Cost (B)	32	63	34	6

Note: (B) Barry; (P) T. K. Park; (S) Schamber.; VI—very important, I—important, NI—not important, DK—don't know.

When Research Is Conducted

Evaluative criteria in this section were taken from the findings of T. K. Park (1992) and Barry (1993). Overall, participants in the current study found all criteria important or very important, with the exception of those about the author, and perceptions about journals. Following are the criteria supporting discussions from Barry and T. K. Park with current study findings.

Previous Experience

The user's previous experience falls into T. K. Park's internal (experience) context category. T. K. Park's findings support the assumption that

> an individual researcher's experience and perceptions about journals, authors, and their previous works, and affiliated academic programs or institutions seem to influence the decision. When the user's perception about the journal is marginal, his or her previous association with the author or the author's affiliated academic program or institution tends to support a decision. (p. 107)

T. K. Park reported six instances in her research where the previous experience proved to be critical to the interviewees' selecting citations for use. Nearly 93 percent of those responding in the current study reported that "previous experience" was either very important or important.

Perceptions about the Author and *Status of Author* (Author name)

Perceptions about the author and status of author falls into T. K. Park's interpretation of citation context. "A citation is considered to represent certain characteristics of a document" (p. 93). "A citation can be regarded as a surrogate of a document, however, [T. K. Park's] findings were able to show a much broader and deeper meaning underlying the relationship" (p. 157).

> The author's status plays a distinctive role in the citation and may influence the selection decision without any interconnections within a citation. A prominent, famous scholar in the field tends to become an independent source of decision regardless of the subject matter. An individual's perception about the author of a citation influences the decision of acceptance or rejection. An individual's previous connec-

tion with an author seems to contribute to evoke the interest of the user. (p. 97)

Conversely, a citation on the subject might be rejected if an individual's perception of the author is poor. (p. 98)

T. K. Park reported on three instances in her sample where the author's status, and/or perceptions about the author were the deciding criteria in interpreting a citation. The status of the author was very important or important to nearly 61 percent of the sample in the current study, and not important to more than a quarter (26.24 percent). More than 7 percent responded that they did not know this criteria. In the current study, perceptions about the author were nearly divided with 48.93 percent believing it was important, and almost 10 percent less believing it was not. This could be explained by the academic status of the sample. The majority of the sample are undergraduates and, therefore, may not have been exposed to in-depth subject area authors to the point of name recognition.

Perceptions about Journals (Journal name and document type).

This criteria falls into T. K. Park's interpretation of the citation context as well.

The quality of the publication influences the selection process and may become a sole source for negative or positive decisions. The user's knowledge and perception about the journal and its status in the field help formulate the decision. (p. 99)

The user's discrimination about the type of document was illustrated in his or her perception about the value of the information. (p. 100)

T. K. Park reported one instance where the interviewee mentioned perceptions about the journal when interpreting the citation. Nearly 71 percent in the current study reported that their perceptions about journals were important or very important. Less than a quarter reported that these perceptions were not important. Again, it is presumed that most undergraduates have not been exposed to specific subject areas to the extent that they are familiar with journals and their importance within particular fields.

Perceptions about Search Quality and *Quality vs. Quantity*

Search quality perceptions fall into T. K. Park's external (search) context category. Quality vs. quantity is an amalgamation of the researcher's experience and T. K. Park's search quality perception.

> An individual's general perception about the search seems to affect the attitude toward selecting a citation. For example, when the user perceives a search to be incomplete, the user tends to select key citations that are very recent and to rely on them to lead him or her into further directions in solving information problems. (p. 118)

T. K. Park reported two instances where this criteria was critical in the decision to accept a citation based on the interpretation. "Perceptions of search quality" was deemed important by more than half the current sample, nearly 60 percent and very important by less than 30 percent. "Quality vs. quantity" was split between very important and important at 47.51 percent and 40.42 percent respectively.

Priority of Information Needs

This category falls into T. K. Park's external (search) context category.

> An individual's priority in terms of the situation of information need and use seems to influence the decision process. The degree of importance, scarcity of information and the current need tend to play a role in the situation. The need situation may take priority over the quality of information. (p. 120)

There were four instances reported from T. K. Park's sample where the priority of information needs was the deciding factor in citation interpretation. Current study findings reveal that the majority of respondents (92.19 percent) believed the "priority of information needs" was either very important or important.

Where You Are in the Search Process (Stage of research)

This category falls into T. K. Park's external (search) context category.

> The research stage and the degree of focus of the individual's problem area seem to result in differences in approaching the selection and interpretation of a citation. (p. 121)

There were four instances reported in T. K. Park's findings where this criteria was of critical importance. "Where you are in the search process" was believed to be either very important or important by 77.30 percent of those responding, and not important to nearly 40 percent.

The End Product

This category falls into T. K. Park's external (search) context category.

> An individual showed a different approach in selecting a citation because of his or her expected end product of research. For example, there are differences in time allocation or interest in the timeliness of the material based on whether an individual's research product is a dissertation, a report for the program sponsor, or a journal article. (p. 122)

The end product was important criteria in two instances in T. K. Park's research. This criteria received significant numbers in the current study, with all but two individuals choosing very important or important.

Perception of Information Available on Chosen Topic

This category falls into T. K. Park's external (search) context category.

> The perception about the information available in the problem area seems to influence the decisions. (p. 119)

This criteria was noted in two instances in T. K. Park's research. Nearly 61 percent of those responding in the current study reported that this perception was important and almost 30 percent believed it was very important.

Time Constraints and Relationship with Author

Barry (1993) placed these criteria in the group of Quality categories which "pertains more to the situational factors affecting the user" (p. 153). Time constraints is defined as "the extent to which time constraints are a factor in the respondent's decision to pursue or not pursue information" (p. 110), and relationship with author is defined as "the respondent has a personal or professional relationship with the author of the document" (p. 109).

Barry's research produced five instances where time was the critical criteria. "Time restraints" was split almost evenly between very important and important, with 46.80 percent and 43.99 percent respectively in the current study. Barry identified four instances in her findings where relationship with the author was reported as being important. "Relationship with author" was not deemed important by more than 57 percent, and, as expected with the demographics of the current sample, nearly a quarter responded that they did not know.

Characteristics about the Article

The majority of these criteria were taken from T. K. Park's interpretation of a citation category. Students were asked to respond to title, style of title, status of author, and quality of publication (journal).

Title and *Style of Title*

> The title plays a leading role in understanding the citation itself and becomes a major property facilitating the understanding of the subject matter of a citation. The user's concern with the title is with key terms that alert the user to the area of interest in the research problem. (p. 93)

> When the words in the title represent the subject matter of a user's information need well conceptually, the title becomes a sole decision source. . . . The understanding of the title of a citation seems to come from an individual's subject knowledge in the problem area. (p. 94)

> The readability of the title and the usage of language can be reasons for rejection in the selection process. (p. 96)

T. K. Park's research identified sixteen instances where the title was important, and an additional four instances where the style of the title was critical in citation interpretation. Nearly 25 percent of the current sample responded that the title was not important. Conversely, more than 70 percent deemed it very important or important. The style of the title was considered not important by 63.12 percent of those responding, important by nearly 30 percent, and very important by less than 7 percent.

Quality of Publication (journal) (Source quality)

Barry defined source quality as "general standards of quality that are predicted based on a source of the document" (p. 109). This criteria was noted in eleven instances by interviewees in Barry's study. In the current study, this criteria was found to be very important by nearly 42 percent, and important by almost 44 percent of the current sample.

What Is in the Article

Characteristics about the information contained in the article identified as relevant for this study included accuracy, currency, specificity, geographic proximity of subject, verifiability, clarity, and information provided was new. All of the criteria in this section were taken from Schamber's (1991) research with the exception of information provided was new, which was taken from T. K. Park (1992).

Accuracy

Schamber defined accuracy as "the information was accurate, usually in the sense of agreement, between a forecast and actual weather conditions." Keywords taken from responses to Schamber's questionnaire included accurate, correct, right, true, and valid (p. 115). Schamber reported forty-three instances of accuracy being identified as an important criteria. Accuracy was deemed very important by more than 80 percent of those responding in the current study, and nearly 17 percent felt it was important. None of the participants selected the not important or don't know categories.

Currency

Currency was defined as "the information was up-to-date or timely," and keywords included current, recent, latest, immediate, and up-to-date (Schamber 1991, p. 116). Schamber's research identified 114 instances from 27 respondents for this criteria, which included time frame as a keyword. Nearly 60 percent of the current sample felt that this criteria was very important and almost 35 percent selected important.

Specificity

Specificity was defined as "the information was specific to respondent's need; had sufficient detail or depth." Keywords listed included specific, exact, precise, focused, concise, detailed, pertinent, in-depth, and complete (Schamber 1991, p. 116). Eighty-four instances were reported by Schamber for specificity as a criteria, including summary/interpretation and variety/voluntary in its definition. Almost 45 percent of the current sample felt this criteria was very important and 43.97 percent selected important.

Geographic Proximity of Subject

Schamber defined this criteria as "the information covered a certain geographic area relative to user's location (usually near user's location or destination), or just covered a desired area." Keywords included area, region, location, altitude, feet, miles, U.S., national, and Canada (p. 117). Ninety-six instances from twenty-seven respondents were recorded by Schamber for this criteria. Nearly 32 percent of the current sample selected not important for this criteria. Conversely, nearly 60 percent deemed this criteria important or very important. Only 10 of the respondents selected "don't know."

Verifiability

Verifiability was defined by Schamber as "other source(s) of weather information were also consulted or available, usually for purposes of comparison." Keywords listed are compared, and double-checked (p. 120). One hundred and three instances, including thirty-nine for source agreement as a keyword, were reported for this criteria in Schamber's study. A majority of the sample (85.81 percent) in this study selected very important or important for this criteria. Only nine of the participants did not deem it important, and three selected "don't know."

Clarity

Schamber defined clarity as "information was presented in a way that was clear; that took little effort to read and understand, or to learn to read," with keywords such as clear, confusing, understandable, easy, hard (p. 120). Schamber further defined clarity as follows: verbal clarity—"written or spoken language was clear and well-organized. It used simple terms instead of jargon, or used jargon the respondent could understand" (p. 120); and visual clarity—"visual display was clear, easy to follow, well-organized. Usually refers to map or graphic, occasionally to text layout" (p. 121). Thirty-four instances were recorded by Schamber for this criteria including nineteen for verbal clarity and eight for visual clarity and the remaining seven for clarity. All current study participants with the exception of one, who selected not important, felt this criteria was either important or very important.

Information Provided was New (New information; in the problem context)

T. K. Park (1992) included this criteria in her problem (content) context category and noted, "The newly received information can stimulate the user's internal state of information need by facilitating new ideas, new directions, or stimulating curiosity" (p. 138). T. K. Park reported five instances of this criteria in her study. In the current study, nearly 80 percent (78.72 percent) felt this criteria was very important or important. Less than 15 percent (14.18 percent) selected not important for this item.

Where the Article Came From

Criteria in this section were taken from the findings of Schamber and Barry.

Accessibility and *Reliability*

Schamber defined accessibility as "source was both available and easy to use; generally convenient. Little effort or cost was required for access and operation." Availability, usability, and affordability fall under accessibility in Schamber's findings (p. 118). Reliability was defined as "respondent trusted, believed, relied on, or had confidence in source and information from source; source was reputable." Expertise, directly observed, source confidence, and consistency fall under this criteria (p. 117). Schamber reported fifty-two instances of accessibility, including thirty-eight for availability, eight for usability, and two for affordability. Reliability was recorded 107 times, including 48 for reliability, 34 for expertise, 13 for directly observed, 4 for source confidence and 8 for consistency. The majority of the participants in the current study felt that both accessibility and reliability were either important (96 percent) or very important (121.98 percent).

Source Novelty

Barry, reporting on ten instances of this criteria, defined source novelty as "The extent to which a source of the document is novel to the respondent," with phrases and keywords such as: "[this source is] unfamiliar, unknown, new" (p. 109). Nearly 20 percent of the respondents felt that source novelty was very important, 41.13 percent felt it was important, almost a quarter did not feel it was important (24.82 percent), and nearly 11 percent responded that they did not know.

Document Novelty (Stimulus document novelty)

Barry defined this criteria as "the extent to which the stimulus document itself is novel to the respondent," and reported ten instances of this criteria. Keywords and phrases listed include this document is unfamiliar, unknown, new, one I didn't know about, one I knew about, one I've read (p. 109). This criteria received results similar to source novelty with 22.69 percent selecting very important, 44.68 percent important, 24.11 percent not important and fifteen individuals selected the don't know category.

Cost

This criteria falls under Barry's access category, where she reported two instances where it had been specifically mentioned. Since accessibility was already included as a criteria, cost was included here. It is defined by Barry as "The extent to which there is cost involved in obtaining a copy of the document" (p. 110). This criteria was considered very important by less than 23 percent of the sample, and important by nearly 45 percent. Nearly a quarter did not think it was important; only six individuals (4.25 percent) responded in the don't know category.

Summary and Discussion

Research Question 4: What are the attitudes and perceptions of college-level students about pre-identified relevance evaluative criteria?

Discussion: Twenty-seven relevance judgment criteria were placed into four categories and students were asked to respond in terms of the importance of the criteria to them when selecting articles for research purposes. Based on the sample demographics, findings were rather predictable. Obvious and readily identifiable criteria such as previous experience, search quality, quality vs. quantity, end products, time constraints, journal quality, accuracy, currency, specificity, verifiability, clarity, new information, accessibility, and reliability were all considered either very important or important to the majority of the respondents.

Less obvious criteria that appear to become more important as students progress and begin significant exploration into specific subject areas received smaller numbers in some of the same categories as mentioned above or were not considered important—cost, document and source novelty, geographic proximity of subject, title, article, and journal and author qualities and perceptions.

The inclusion of the "don't know" category appears to have decreased the tendency to guess. This assumption is based on the fact that there are numbers in this column, some significant, but all categories, except clarity, and accuracy, received at least one score for "don't know."

Overall, the students attitudes about the previously identified criteria taken from Barry (1993), T. K. Park (1992), and Schamber (1991) were positive in that the criteria identified by subjects in the dissertations were echoed and confirmed by education students at the Targeted University.

Testing the Model—Statistical Analysis

Using Statistical Package for the Social Sciences (SPSS) correlation coefficients were computed for each of the five elements in the model (excluding demographics). As a result of the inability to quantify the relevance findings for this study, the original model was reviewed and adapted to reflect the statistically viable nature of the relationships between all other elements. Figure 4.1 shows the adapted model with all pairwise relationships depicting the correlational nature of the model elements, with the exception of relevance.

T-tests were computed to determine if the means were statistically significant at the selected probability level of .05 or a 95 percent confidence interval. Means and t-tests were also computed for each of the model elements controlling for gender (male and female), and academic status (undergraduate and graduate). A primary concern in the data analysis was to test the model's assumption about the hypothesized relationships.

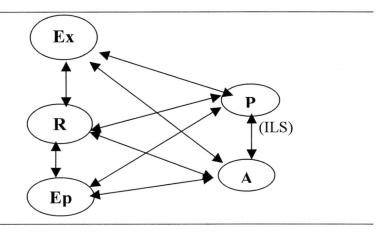

Figure 4.1. Adapted model of the element relationship to information literacy skills (ILS).

Covariance Analysis

The model offered two opportunities for statistical analysis. One was covariance recovery and the other was regression analysis. Based on covariance analysis, figure 4.2 shows a bar graph depiction of the correlation coefficients; table 4.18 shows the coefficients numerically.

Figure 4.2 reveals the five elements are correlated and statistically significant, with a 95 percent confidence interval, as all probability values are less than or equal to .001 (see table 4.18). The size of confidence intervals are based on the sample size. Using correlation coefficient tables of confidence intervals from *Basic Statistical Tables* (1971), table 4.18 reveals all correlations are significant with intervals that are approximately plus or minus .14. Figure 4.3 shows the correlation coefficients computed for each of the pairwise relationships for the adapted model—figure 4.1.

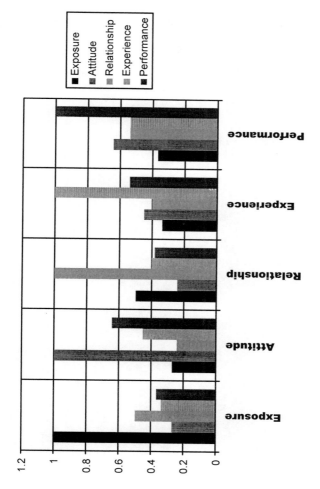

Figure 4.2. Bar graph of the correlation coefficients of the five elements.

Table 4.18. Correlation coefficients and p-values of five elements

		Experience	Relationship	Performance	Attitude
		Correlation (Sample) P-value (95% CI)	Correlation (Sample) P-value (95% CI)	Correlation (Sample) P-value (95% CI)	Correlation (Sample) P-value (95% CI)
Exposure	1.0000 (149) P=	.3375 (149) P= .000 (.20, 50)	.4967 (149) P= .000 (.62, .37)	.3668 (149) P= .000 (.51, .22)	.2711 (149) P= .001 (.42, .12)
Experience		1.0000 (149) P=	.4002 (149) P= .000 (.54, .25)	.5398 (149) P= .000 (.66, .42)	.4495 (149) P= .001 (.58, .31)
Relationship			1.0000 (149) P=	.3821 (149) P=.000 (.52, .23)	.2409 (149) P=.003 (.40, .08)
Performance				1.0000 (149) P=	.6416 (149) P=.000 (.74, .54)
Attitude					1.0000 (149) P=

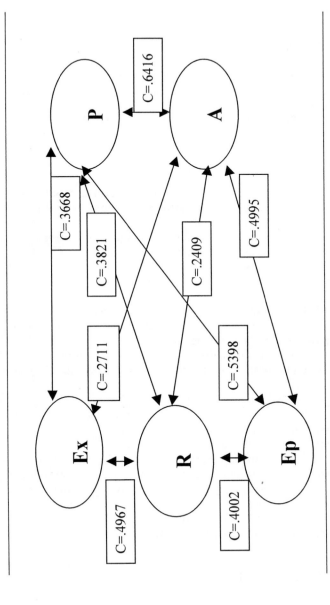

Figure 4.3. Correlation coefficients of five elements of the model.

In relation to the hypotheses of this study, the results of the covariance analysis will be examined next.

Hypotheses: Original Model

Hypothesis 1: If the attitudinal component of information literacy skills is high, then the performance component of information literacy skills will be high.
Discussion: The findings of this study support the hypothesis presumptions that attitudinal and performance components of information literacy skills are correlated. There was a correlation coefficient of .64, significant at the .05 level (see figure 4.3).

Hypothesis 2: If the level of exposure in a college-level student is found to be high, then the measure of the performance component of the information literacy skills will be high.
Discussion: Figure 4.3 and table 4.18 show that the correlation coefficient between exposure and performance is .37, significant at the .05 level. This hypothesis was supported by the data. Figure 4.2 shows the relationship between these two elements visually.

Hypothesis 3: If the level of experience in a college-level student is found to be high, then the measure of the performance component of the information literacy skills will be high.
Discussion: There was a correlation coefficient of .54, significant at the .05 level (see figure 4.3), thus, this hypothesis was supported by the data.

Hypothesis 4: If the strength of the relationship between students and faculty is found to be high, then the measure of the performance component of the information literacy skills will be high.
Discussion: The correlation coefficient between the relationship between students and faculty and the performance component of information literacy skills is .38. This hypothesis was supported by the data.

Hypothesis 5: If the level of exposure is found to be high in college-level students, then the measure of the attitudinal component of information literacy skills will be high.
Discussion: There was a correlation coefficient of .27, significant at the .05 level (see figure 4.3). This hypothesis was supported by the data.

Hypothesis 6: If the level of experience is found to be high in college-level students, then the measure of the attitudinal component of information literacy skills will be high.

Discussion: The correlation coefficient between experience and attitude is .45, significant at the .05 level (see figure 4.3). This hypothesis was supported by the data.

Hypothesis 7: If the strength of the relationship between students and faculty is found to be high in college-level students, then the measure of the attitudinal component of information literacy skills will be high.

Discussion: There was a correlation coefficient between relationship with faculty and attitude of .24, significant at the .05 level (see figure 4.3). This hypothesis was supported by the data.

In addition to the knowledge that the five variables are positively correlated, further statistical analyses were conducted to understand the nature and extent of the relationships. Multiple regression analyses were conducted to explore the standardized regression coefficients associated with each predicting variable within each equation. The regression statements can be expressed as thus:

Exposure + Relationship with Faculty + Experience as predictor of Performance

Exposure + Relationship with Faculty + Experience as predictor of Attitude

The intent of these additional calculations was to determine the extent of the relationship with the three variables and how they independently affect the performance and attitudinal components of information literacy.

Performance and attitude were used as dependent variables in regression analyses. Using SPSS for Unix, the following were computed for the regression analyses. The independent variables were exposure (E_1), relationship with faculty (R), and experience (E_2). Table 4.19 summarizes the results of the regression procedures.

Table 4.19. Regression analyses

Independent Variables	Standardized Regression Coefficients			
	Performance	Sig.	Attitude	Sig.
Exposure	.154924	.051	.127576	.140
Relationship with Faculty	.131014	.108	.01686	.841
Experience	.434046	<.001	.399345	.001
R^2	.34171		.21835	
Adjusted R^2	.32809		.20218	
F	25.08955	p<.001	13.50174	p<.001

The results reveal that experience and exposure are significant independent predictors of performance. The only significant independent predictor of attitude was experience.

Figure 4.4 is a restructured model which accommodates the findings of the regression analyses.

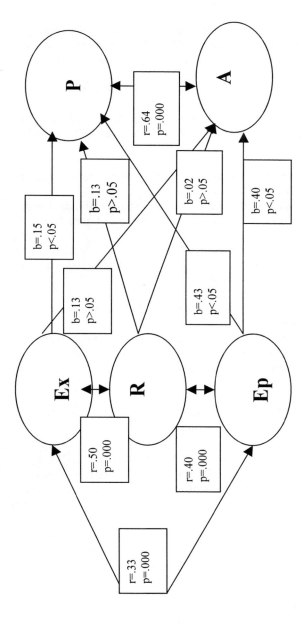

Figure 4.4. Restructured theoretical model based on regression analyses.

Hypotheses: Revised Model

As a result of the regression analyses, the data reveals additional hypotheses based on the model element relationships. Two of these hypotheses are similar to the regression statements presented earlier.

Hypothesis 8: Exposure, relationship with faculty, and experience have a direct and independent effect on performance.
Discussion: Only experience and exposure had direct and independent effects on performance, therefore, this hypothesis was only partially corroborated (see figure 4.3).

Hypothesis 9: Exposure, relationship with faculty, and experience have a direct and independent effect on attitude.
Discussion: Only experience was significantly related to attitude, therefore, this hypothesis was also partially corroborated (see figure 4.4).

Hypothesis 10: Performance and attitude are significantly correlated.
Discussion: This hypothesis was strongly supported by the data, with a reported correlation of .64 (see figure 4.4).

Hypothesis 11: Exposure, relationship with faculty and experience are significantly correlated.
Discussion: This hypothesis was strongly supported in the data with the following correlations being reported: exposure and relationship with faculty—.50; relationship with faculty and experience—.40; experience and exposure—.33.

Research Question 1: What are the sociological and psychological factors which affect information literacy skills?

Discussion: In conducting the review of the literature section for this study, five elements were identified from the library science and education literature which were believed to affect information literacy skills. Those elements were found to be attitude (how do students feel about information literacy skills?); performance (how do college-level students perform when interpreting or performing information literacy skills?); relationship with faculty (what is the nature of the relationship between faculty and college-level students?); exposure (what is the level of exposure the student has to the information environment?); and experience (what is the level of experience the college-level student has in the information environment?). These five elements were statistically analyzed based on quantifiable data collected from the sample.

Research Question 2: What is the extent of the relationship between the sociological and psychological factors in the information literacy framework?

Discussion: Under the original model (see figure 4.3), correlation coefficients revealed that the relationship with faculty element was important in the model. Under the adapted model (see figure 4.4), the effects of relationship with faculty on performance and attitude is not direct, but, mediated through the effects on exposure and experience. Relatively speaking, experience may be the lead predictor of performance and attitude followed, perhaps, by exposure.

Summary

Statistical analyses were conducted on the data in order to determine whether there were correlations between the elements of the adapted model. Hypotheses one through seven, and research questions one and two were supported and, thus, accepted based on the resulting coefficient correlations.

Regression analysis produced four additional hypotheses, two of which were accepted based on the resulting analysis. The other two hypotheses were partially corroborated based on the data. Experience and exposure were found to be significant independent predictors of performance; and experience was found to be the only significant predictor of attitude. Relationship with faculty affects performance and attitude through its effect on exposure and experience.

Additional Statistical Analysis

T-tests were conducted to determine if there were any significant differences between gender (female and male), and academic status (undergraduates and graduates) in their responses to the five elements.

Gender

Table 4.20 shows the results of the calculations performed on each of the elements controlling for gender. These calculations include means, mean differences, and p-values. It should be noted that females scored higher more often than males in four of the element areas (exposure, attitude, experience, performance). In all areas except performance, there was no significant difference between the two groups. Female and male responses did not differ significantly to responses in the exposure, attitude, relationship with faculty or experience sections. Figure 4.5 shows a bar graph rendering of the mean difference between males and females in responses to items in the performance section. All bar graphs are scaled from the lowest to the highest possible index score for the section depicted. All other elements with no significant differences are represented in figures A.5 through A.8, appendix A.

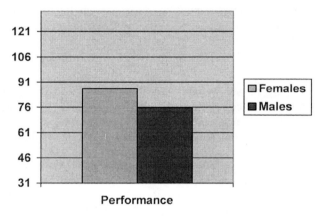

Figure 4.5. Mean difference in gender—performance.

The mean difference between males and females for the performance section is 11.4221, with a p-value of .042 which is less than .05, thus, this difference is significant with a confidence interval of 95 percent.

Table 4.20. T-tests for Independent Samples of Gender

Variable	Number of Cases						
	Gender	n	Mean	SD	SE of Mean	Mean Difference	p value
Exposure	Female	86	08.9884	7.936	0.856	00.9666	.502
	Male	46	08.0217	7.724	1.139		
Attitude	Female	86	36.0814	12.664	1.436	01.0162	.672
	Male	46	35.0652	13.921	2.053		
Relationship with Faculty	Female	86	04.3488	03.165	0.341	-00.1294	.832
	Male	46	04.4783	03.638	0.536		
Experience	Female	86	04.5000	02.310	0.249	00.5870	.187
	Male	46	03.9130	02.615	0.386		
Performance	Female	86	87.1395	27.888	3.007	11.4221	.042
	Male	46	75.7174	34.817	5.134		

Academic Status

T-tests were also performed to determine whether there were any differences between undergraduates and graduates in responses to the five
elements. Table 4.21 shows the results of those calculations. On the
elements of exposure, relationship with faculty, and experience, undergraduate answers differed significantly from graduates. The only element in which undergraduates scored higher than graduates was attitude.

Figures 4.6 through 4.8 below show the mean differences in bar
column form for exposure (-3.0720), relationship with faculty (-1.5388),
and experience (-1.1266). The highest and lowest index score possible
for the three areas (exposure, experience, relationship) is represented in
the Y-axis in each of the graphs. Mean differences for attitude and performance were not significant with p-values of .543 and .323 respectively.

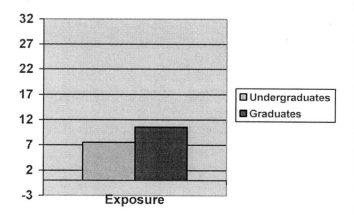

Figure 4.6. Mean difference in academic status—exposure.

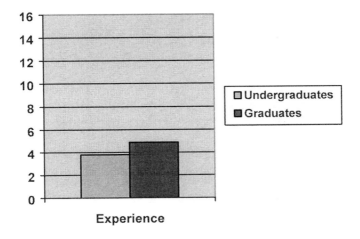

Figure 4.7. Mean difference in academic status—experience.

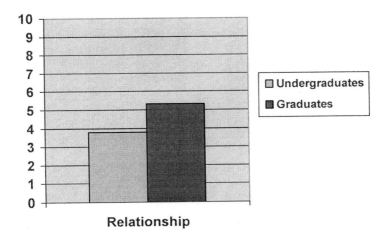

Figure 4.8. Mean difference in academic status—relationship with faculty.

Table 4.21. T-tests for Independent Samples of Academic Status

Number of Cases

Variable	Academic Status	n	Mean	SD	SE of Mean	Mean Difference	p value
Exposure	Undergraduate	73	07.5205	07.638	0.894	-3.0720	.033
	Graduate	54	10.5926	08.316	1.132		
Attitude	Undergraduate	73	36.3288	12.805	1.499	1.4028	.543
	Graduate	54	34.9259	12.822	1.745		
Relationship with Faculty	Undergraduate	73	03.7945	03.050	0.357	-1.5388	.012
	Graduate	54	05.3333	03.752	0.511		
Experience	Undergraduate	73	03.7808	02.287	0.268	-1.1266	.008
	Graduate	54	04.9074	02.373	0.323		
Performance	Undergraduate	73	81.2740	32.281	3.778	-5.3927	.323
	Graduate	54	86.6667	27.260	3.710		

Summary

Statistical analyses were conducted on the data in order to determine whether there were correlations between the elements of the model. Hypotheses one through seven were supported, and research questions one and two were answered based on the resulting coefficient correlations. Regression analyses revealed that experience and exposure are independent predictors of performance, and attitude is affected by experience. Relationship with faculty has an indirect effect on performance and attitude, mediated through its effect on exposure and experience.

Additional statistical testing revealed that although females scored higher more often on four of the element items than males; with the exception of performance, there was no significant difference between the two groups. Academic status was a consideration when responding to items in exposure, experience, and relationship with faculty elements.

Notes

1. The text of the letter to the faculty and to students participating in the study can be found in the Appendices of the original dissertation (Neely 2000, pp. 283-86).
2. The survey instrument can be found in the Appendices of the original dissertation (Neely 2000, pp. 247-49).
3. Respondents did not have access to the research questions during the pilot.
4. The Researcher's home University Library uses the Netscape browser primarily.

Chapter 5

Research Summary and Conclusions

The purpose of this research was to investigate the sociological and psychological factors, as evidenced in the literature, that are believed to affect college-level students' ability to make relevance judgments; determine the extent of the relationship between sociological and psychological factors in the information literacy framework; collect information about the attitudes of college-level students toward Doyle's (1992) ten information literacy skills; and identify college-level students' attitudes and perceptions about previously identified relevance/evaluative criteria. It also investigated the following research questions and hypotheses:

Research Questions

1. What are the sociological and psychological factors which affect information literacy skills?
2. What is the extent of the relationship between sociological and psychological factors in the information literacy framework?

3. What are the attitudes and perceptions of college-level students about Doyle's (1992) ten information literacy skills?
4. What are the attitudes and perceptions of college-level students about pre-identified relevance evaluative criteria?

Hypotheses

1. If the attitudinal component of information literacy skills is high, then the performance component of information literacy skills will be high.
2. If the level of exposure in a college-level student is found to be high, then the measure of the performance component of information literacy skills will be high.
3. If the level of experience in a college-level student is found to be high, then the measure of the performance component of information literacy skills will be high.
4. If the strength of the relationship between students and faculty is found to be high, then the measure of the performance component of information literacy skills will be high.
5. If the level of exposure is found to be high in college-level students, then the measure of the attitudinal component of information literacy skills will be high.
6. If the level of experience is found to be high in college-level students, then the measure of the attitudinal component of information literacy skills will be high.
7. If the strength of the relationship between students and faculty is found to be high, then the measure of the attitudinal component of information literacy skills will be high.

In order to complete this investigation, the study adapted and administered the Morner Test of Library Research Skills developed and validated by Morner in her 1993 dissertation, *A Test of Library Research Skills for Education Doctoral Students*. The resulting instrument, The Neely Test of Relevance, Evaluation, and Information Literacy Attitudes, was administered to 144 undergraduate and graduate students enrolled in required courses in the School of Education at the Targeted University. Morner's instrument was selected because a review of the literature revealed no other instrument had been developed, nor had any empirical research of this nature been conducted that contained the information literacy skills represented in the research literature.

Other instruments developed for information literacy research (see Daragan and Stevens 1996; Maughan 1994), or containing information literacy components (see Libutti 1991; Ochs et al. 1991; South Seattle Community College 1993) upon review, proved to be by definition, information literacy-related, however, in content, these instruments were inconsistent, and not representative of the Doyle (1992) skills, nor the ALA (1989) definition. In general, they were inadequate for the current study. Morner's instrument, although developed for doctoral education students, could be adapted largely intact, with minimal changes for the current sample demographics. Much of the content was maintained and expanded upon in the current study, aided by an extensive review of the literature.

Summary of Principle Study Findings

A review of the research and professional library science and education literature revealed the sociological and psychological factors that are believed to affect college-level students evaluative judgments to be exposure, relationship with faculty, experience, and the performance and attitudinal aspects of information literacy. Covariance statistical analyses revealed that all were positively correlated. Additional statistical analysis using regression analyses showed that performance was directly affected by experience and exposure, and that attitude was directly affected by experience. Relationship with faculty indirectly affects performance and attitude. This effect is mediated through its effects on exposure and experience.

Overall, findings in all model elements reveal significant evidence that supports findings from the previously reported research in the review of the literature section. Students at all levels (undergraduate, masters, doctoral) are receiving minimal levels of exposure in each of the eight formats queried; and this is perceived as adequate. Library anxiety remains an acute problem that is apparently not being addressed.

With the exception of the demographic section which provided specific data about the sample itself, the self-reported comfort levels and attitudinal findings indicated a clear over-assumption of information literacy skills and abilities, specifically evaluation. These over-assumptions were confirmed when students responded to items which required them to demonstrate their knowledge in the performance and experience sections. Responses to the self-report items in the attitude section contrasted sharply with items in experience and performance which depicted specific information literacy skills. Unfortunately, it appears, students are unaware of the limited or lack of skills they possess and, also, unaware of what they do not know. This observation echoes and confirms those made previously in research by Damko

(1990). This may be a result of where the majority of the sample first acquired library research skills—high school, on their own, or in elementary or grade school. There is evidence of empirical research which reports that high school library skills are not transferable to college (Kester 1994), and also that the only skill transferable from secondary school is the ability to consult a librarian (Goodin 1991).

Few faculty members at the Targeted University's School of Education are contributing to the information literacy development of their students in the classroom environment; although students are still expected to possess research and information literacy skills and are assigned coursework accordingly. Few from the sample have worked with faculty in a one-on-one environment; however, this could be a function of the sample makeup being predominantly undergraduate in nature.

In terms of the students' attitudes about information literacy skills, the data gathered and disseminated here will contribute to the published literature in this area, which currently consists of one (H. Morrison 1997) study. In querying the students' attitudes about the ten (Doyle 1992) information literacy skills, in each instance, 50 percent or more of the students reported being comfortable or very comfortable with the skills. However, when viewed with additional current study data (performance and experience), the findings further confirm the notion that self-reporting alone is not a viable method for determining reliable student attitudes.

Performance findings were, in general, not favorable, signaling a need for increased instruction in the area of information evaluation and critical thinking skills. Findings in this section were also, in general, not comparable as a result of the limited empirical published research on information literacy, specifically, the evaluative skills of college-level students. The decision to include an "I don't know" option to experience section items appears to have eliminated the tendency for students to guess in this, the only section where survey items required a correct answer. Experience findings confirmed suspicions represented in the literature that students at all levels are lacking in basic library research skills.

Responses to the previously identified relevance query items confirm the importance of these criteria from the perspective of the student (researcher). The items are also self-report in nature but when viewed with the findings of Schamber (1991), T. K. Park (1992), and Barry (1993), provide previously unavailable data from this population (education students) about how and why they make relevance judgments. With this knowledge of what criteria are important to education students, education related bibliographic instruction sessions and programs can be tailored and focused in order to enhance the areas students have indicated as important.

Conclusions

Model Driven Conclusions

Based on the statistical analyses performed using regression analysis, the following conclusions derived from the model are noted for this study:

1. College-level students are not being exposed to library and information literacy skills environments; when there is exposure, it is limited predominantly to "1 to 2 times," currently, and in general.
2. In general, college-level students are using computers for a variety of reasons including word-processing/spreadsheets; email/chat rooms; and the Internet/World Wide Web.
3. Although the majority of the sample reported feeling frustrated with libraries; more than half of the students also reported being comfortable or very comfortable with library databases; and, 93 percent of the sample reported using computers in libraries.
4. Attitudes about (Doyle 1992) information literacy skills, based on comfort levels are overwhelmingly positive in all areas; however, when these self-report findings are analyzed in conjunction with additional survey data from the performance and experience sections, it is apparent that students greatly overestimated confidence levels.
5. Students in the sample reported limited information literacy skills interaction with current faculty members; confirming that few faculty members participate in library research and information literacy skills modeling for students in the classroom environment and in formalized one-on-one interactions (i.e., teaching practicums, master's thesis, dissertation advising).
6. Data gathered in the experience section, overwhelmingly confirming previously reported research, found that students at all levels are not familiar with basic library research skills or search strategies, nor leading education resources.
7. Overall, college-level students are not equipped to make evaluative judgments about information in a variety of formats used in research projects for a variety of end products; however, they may not be aware of this inability.

8. The effectiveness of evaluative judgments made by participants appear to be overrated when self-reported; a finding confirmed by subsequent survey items.
9. In general, participants were not comfortable with previously identified criteria which denoted specific knowledge of or a relationship with authors, source (journal) perception, or geographic proximity of subject.
10. Gender was not a factor in response to survey elements except on performance (evaluation) items where the mean female score was significantly higher than males.
11. Academic status was a factor in response to survey elements of exposure, experience, and relationship with faculty.
12. Automated survey testing appears to decrease manual test taking time by nearly eight minutes.

Weakness of the Study

Sample

The lack of a considerable Ph.D. student and freshmen contingency in the sample did not allow adequate or generalizable comparisons between these students and the remaining groups in the sample.

Recommendations for Future Research

The research conducted by Morner (1993) provided the foundation for the current instrument development, and the current study replicated and extended the 1993 study. However, the current study raises a number of critical issues in light of the new data, much of which had not been explored before.

1. The faculty/student relationship is a critical one in the development of library research and information literacy skills in students, programs and, also, in collaborative efforts where the success of the students is the desired outcome. The findings of this study indicate the relationship with the faculty element affects the attitude and performance aspects of information literacy skills, through its effect on experience and exposure. Additional research in this area must be conducted in order to determine the most advantageous ways for faculty to contribute to the experience and enhance the exposure level of college-level students.

2. More research is needed on the students' perceptions of the nature of the relationship with faculty in order to further clarify the specific role of faculty in information literacy skills development for all students. There is a wealth of evidence from the faculty's perspective; it is time to focus on the students' perspective. Additional research from the perspective of the faculty should focus on faculty behavior and whether they perceive a need for change.

3. Self-assessment alone cannot be considered a valid indicator of student skills and information literacy levels. Additional methods of obtaining and qualifying this invaluable data must be explored and incorporated into information literacy and library research skills assessment tools.

4. Further research is needed to empirically establish tools to assess information literacy levels in a standardized fashion, in order to obtain appropriate and relevant outcomes. The Neely Test should be used, either in parts (elements), or in its entirety, to assess different samples and populations in order to obtain widespread generalizable results that are reliable and valid. The experience section is easily adapted for specific subject areas.

5. Future research on the evaluation skills of students must be conducted in order to substantiate the widely disseminated arguments for and against information literacy. Research in the social sciences is confirmed and validated through replication.

6. Any research on information literacy and evaluative skills must include a discussion of comparable research in other areas, specifically education and information science. Schamber (1991), T. K. Park (1992), and Barry (1993) have made significant inroads in information science with user-based relevance criteria, however, the concept of relevance remains a relatively new construct in library science. There is much work to be done in regard to quantifying the findings of this research on relevance judgments and the evaluative criteria taken directly from users in real-life information seeking situations; as well, there is much to learn from the burgeoning body of user-based relevance studies gathered directly from users in real-life information situations.

7. There is also considerable professional work that has been done in the name of information literacy, but significant, systematic efforts must still be made toward standardizing definition interpretations, and greatly increasing empirical evidence of measurable generalizable outcomes.

8. There is empirical evidence that library anxiety is separate from trait anxiety and the data gathered in this study suggests that computers in libraries may not be a factor. Library anxiety is a real

phenomena which must be addressed and methods for decreasing library anxiety for students of all ages at all levels must be explored and incorporated into existing, and developing library research skills and information literacy programs.

9. Future research on information literacy should consider the Association of College and Research Libraries information literacy competency standards for higher education, which were approved in January of 2000 by the ACRL Task Force on Information Literacy Competency Standards (ACRL 2000).

Future Instrument Development

Instructions for the exposure section should be reviewed for clarity. During testing, some respondents requested clarification for definitions for *in general* and *currently*. This may also have been a function of a hurried, or non reading of the instructions that were included with the instrument. The Neely Test should be reviewed for methods to quantify responses to relevance items in order to further test the model statistically; and, also to investigate further, quantitatively, how and why college students make evaluative judgments. Methods to develop quantitative items from T. K. Park's (1992) problem (content) context also should be explored to address this issue.

Implications

These study findings have widespread implications in library science and education, and also for information science (user-based relevance studies). User (student) input is a valid indicator for the development and restructuring of information literacy and library skills research programs, curricula, and individualized courses. Student attitudes about these skills are an intricate part of the success of these programs and must be included in the development of programs with quantifiable outcomes, thus, contributing to a more efficient and effective program.

Practical Implications

Foremost in conducting further information literacy research are the questions which must be asked based on the theoretical findings of this study:

1. What can faculty, librarians, (instruction) programs, institutions, organizations, professional societies, and others do to

enhance the experience and exposure of students. These factors directly affect the performance component of information literacy skills which affects/contribute to an information literate individual/student.

2. What can faculty, librarians, (instruction) programs, institutions, organizations, professional societies, and others do to enhance the experience of students. This factor directly affects the attitude component of information literacy skills which affects/contribute to an information literate individual/student.

3. How and what can faculty (relationship with) do to enhance the exposure and experience of students? The relationship factor indirectly affects/contributes to an information literate individual/student by directly affecting the exposure and experience factors.

4. What methods can be employed to effectively enhance the experience and exposure of college-level students when relationship with faculty is not a given? Exposure and experience are key to the information literacy of college-level students. What other ways might library faculty and staff contribute to improving these factors when the relationship with faculty element is not a factor in the deliberations?

As the information superhighway continues to make rapid and significant inroads via digital and cable television, WebTV™, radio, multimedia, and personal computers into the K-12 and higher education environments, commercial and private sectors, libraries, and private residences, mass information will continue to increase in complexity and volume, while, simultaneously, becoming a much valued commodity. It is to the benefit of all with stakes in this increasingly information literate environment to acquire the necessary qualitative and quantitative skills to embrace and navigate information in these fast moving and rapid fire times.

Appendix A

Table A.1. General Computer Use

N=136	Computer Use	Percentage Selected
121	E-mail/Chat rooms	88.97
122	Word processing/ Spreadsheets	89.70
99	Searching databases	72.29
120	Internet/World Wide Web	88.23
75	Games/Entertainment	55.14
39	Work-related/ Telecommuting	28.67
2	Other	01.47

Table A.2. Academic status distribution with neutral "3" answers to items 28 and 29.

	Freshmen	Sophomore	Junior	Senior	Master's	Doctoral	Other	Totals
28. More useful/least useful								
Available in a research library	1	4	2	7	6	0	2	22
Indexed in a computer database	0	3	2	8	12	1	0	26
Published in a refereed journal	3	7	11	12	11	0	2	46
Written by university faculty	1	8	6	10	18	2	3	48
Published in a textbook	1	5	5	7	11	1	3	33
Thesis and dissertations	3	11	7	11	21	3	1	57
29. Most likely to include/exclude								
Article available only by interlibrary loan/not available locally	1	4	2	6	9	1	3	26
Full text of article not available locally	1	4	9	6	20	1	3	44
Article too long	2	9	4	12	26	1	4	58
Abstract not included with citation	0	7	8	7	18	1	4	45
Article is too advanced/technical	2	9	5	6	19	0	4	45
Article is too general	2	7	4	11	18	1	2	45

Table A.3. Academic status distribution to items 28 and 29.

28. More useful

	Freshmen	Sophomore	Junior	Senior	Master's	Doctoral	Other	Totals
Available in a research library	3	7	9	18	20	2	2	61
Indexed in a computer database	1	7	7	16	24	2	2	59
Published in a refereed journal	0	2	2	8	16	1	1	30
Written by university faculty	1	0	3	4	5	1	1	15
Published in a textbook	1	4	6	8	9	0	1	29
Thesis and dissertations	0	0	1	1	4	0	1	7

29. Most likely to include

	Freshmen	Sophomore	Junior	Senior	Master's	Doctoral	Other	Totals
Article available only by interlibrary loan/not available locally	0	0	2	3	7	1	0	13
Full text of article not available locally	0	1	2	6	5	1	0	15
Article too long	0	0	1	0	3	0	1	5
Abstract not included with citation	0	2	2	2	1	0	0	7
Article is too advanced/technical	0	0	0	1	2	0	0	3
Article is too general	1	0	0	1	2	0	0	4

Table A.4. Reliable resources and use of Internet article

31. Reliable sources when conducting research

	Percent Choosing
Sources by or recommended by scholars in the subject area	84.17
Published bibliographies, including those located at the end of books and articles	49.64
Sources used by other students and colleagues	52.51
Sources found on the Internet or in on-line databases	67.62
Sources recommended by professors, librarians, and/or teaching assistants	87.76
Conference proceedings or publications by professional associations	50.35
Subject-related review articles	56.83

32. Use an article found on the Internet for research project

	Percent Choosing
Article written and signed by an individual with no known subject-related credentials	8.63
Article written by an individual with a Ph.D.	51.79
Article written by a known scholar	76.97
Article available from a website ending in EDU and/or connected to a school, college, or university	58.99
Article published as part of a proceedings of a professional organization on their website	61.15
Full text of article available	64.02
Article available from a free website or database accessible via the World Wide Web	27.33
Article listed in the syllabus of a professor	78.41

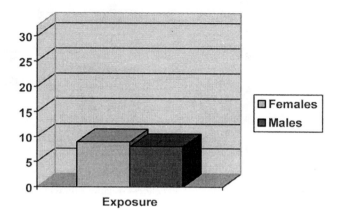

Figure A.1. Mean difference in gender—exposure (.9666)

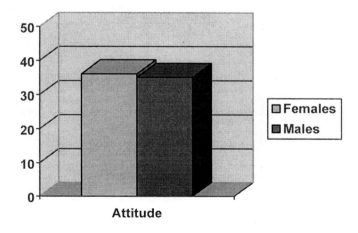

Figure A.2. Mean difference in gender—attitude (1.0162)

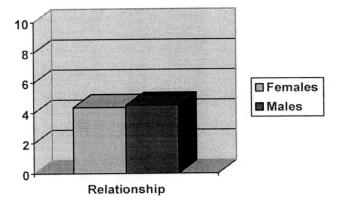

Figure A.3. Mean difference in gender—relationship with faculty (-1294)

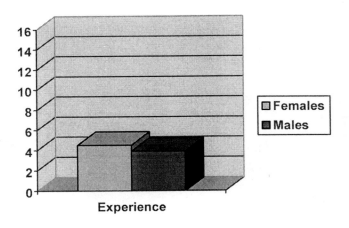

Figure A.4. Mean difference in gender—experience (.5870)

Bibliography

ACRL Task Force on Information Literacy Competency Standards. 2000. Information literacy competency standards for higher education: The final version, approved January 2000. *College and Research Libraries News* 61:207-15.

Alire, Camila A. 1984. A nationwide survey of education doctoral students' attitudes regarding the importance of the library and the need for bibliographic instruction. Ph.D. diss., University of Northern Colorado.

Altan, Susan. 1988. Desperately seeking standards. In *Reaching and Teaching Diverse Library User Groups,* edited by Teresa B. Mensching. Ann Arbor, Mich.: Pieran Press.

American Association of School Librarians. 1997. American Association of School Librarian's new standards due this fall. *School Library Journal* 43:29.

American Association of School Librarians and the National Commission on Libraries and Information Science. 1989. *Information Literacy and Education for the 21st Century. Toward an Agenda for Action.* Leesburg, Va., April 14-16, ERIC, ED 330343.

American Library Association Presidential Committee on Information Literacy. 1989. *Final Report.* Chicago, Ill., ERIC, ED 316074.

Amstutz, Donna D., and Donna L. Whitson. 1997. University faculty and information literacy: Who teaches the students? *Research Strategies* 15:18-25.

Arp, Lori, and Kathleen Kenny. 1990. Vital connections: Composition and BI Theory in the LRC. *New Directions for Community Colleges* 18:13-22.

Arp, Lori, and Lizbeth A. Wilson. 1989. Structures of bibliographic instruction programs: A continuum for planning. *Reference Librarian* 24:25-34.

Barger, Robert R., and Jane Mayo-Chamberlain. 1983. Advisor and advisee issues in doctoral education. *Journal of Higher Education* 54: 407-32.

Bar-Hillel, Yehoshua. 1960. Some theoretical aspects of the mechanization of literature searching. Washington, D.C.: Office of Technical Services. NSF, AD-236 772 and PB-161 547.

Barry, Carol L. 1993. The identification of user relevance criteria and document characteristics: Beyond the topical approach to information retrieval. Ph.D. diss., Syracuse University.

————. 1994. User-defined relevance criteria: An exploratory study. *Journal of the American Society for Information Science* 45:149-59.

Barry, Carol L., and Linda Schamber. 1995. User-defined relevance criteria: A comparison of two studies. In *Proceedings of the 58th Annual Meeting of the American Society for Information Science* 32:103-11.

Baxter, Pam M. 1990. A view of academics' literature search methods: The case of the social sciences and its implications for students. *Serials and Reference Services* 27-28:419-31.

Beghtol, Clare. 1986. Bibliographic classification theory and text linguistics: Aboutness analysis, intertextuality and the cognitive act of classifying documents. *Journal of Documentation* 42:84-113.

Behrens, Shirley J. 1994. A conceptual analysis and historical overview of information literacy. *College and Research Libraries* 55:309-22.

Belkin, Nicholas J. 1980. The problem of "matching" in information retrieval. In *Theory and application of information research:* Proceedings of the 2nd International Research Forum on Information Science, August 36, 1977, edited by Ole H. Harbo and Leif Kajberg. Copenhagen, Denmark; London, England: Mansell, 1980.

Belkin, Nicholas J., Colleen Cool, Adelheit Stein, and Ulrich Thiel. 1995. Cases, scripts, and information seeking strategies: On the design of interactive information retrieval systems. *Expert Systems with Applications* 9:379-95.

Belkin, Nicholas J., and W. Bruce Croft. 1987. Retrieval techniques. In *Annual Review of Information Science and Technology*, Vol. 22, edited by Martha E. Williams. Amsterdam, The Netherlands: Elsevier Science Publishers for the American Society for Information Science.

Benenfeld, Alan R., Pater Kugel, and Richard S. Marcus. 1978. Catalog information and text as indicators of relevance. *Journal of the American Society for Information Science* 29:15-30.

Beyer, William H. 1971. *Basic statistical tables.* Cleveland, Ohio: Chemical Rubber Co.

Biden, Francis W. 1997. United States Government Printing Office. In *The Bowker Annual Library and Book Trade Almanac,* 42nd ed., edited by Dave Bogart. New Providence, N.J.: R. R. Bowker.

Booker, Di., ed. 1992. *Information literacy: The Australian agenda.* Proceedings of a conference conducted by the University of South Australia Library held at Adelaide College of TAFE, 2-4 December, 1992. University of South Australia, Adelaide.

Bookstein, Abraham. 1979. Relevance. *Journal of the American Society for Information Science* 30:269-73.

Bopp, Richard E., and Linda C. Smith, eds. 1995. *Reference and information services: An introduction,* 2nd ed. Englewood, Colo.: Libraries Unlimited.

Boyce, Bert R. 1982. Beyond topicality: A two stage view of relevance and the retrieval process. *Information Processing and Management* 18:105-9.

Branch, Katherine A., and Debra L. Gilchrist. 1996. Library instruction and information literacy in community and technical colleges. *Reference Quarterly* 35:476-83.

Breivik, Patricia Senn. 1977. Resources: The Fourth R. *Community College Frontiers* 5:46-50.

———. 1985. A vision in the making: Putting libraries back in the information society. *American Libraries* 16:723.

———. 1987. Assessing information literacy. Paper presented at Second National Conference in Higher Education, PLACE, June 14-17, 1987.

———. 1989. Politics for closing the gap. *Reference Librarian* 24:5-16.

———. 1992. Education for the information age. *New Directions for Higher Education* 78:5-13.

Breivik, Patricia Senn, and J. A. Senn. 1994. *Information literacy: Educating children for the 21st century.* New York: Scholastic.

Breivik, Patricia Senn, Vicki Hancock, and J. A. Senn. 1998. A progress report on Information Literacy: An update on the American Library Association Presidential Committee on Information Literacy: Final Report. Chicago: American Library Association and the National Forum on Information Literacy. Available from American

Library Association Web site (on-line website) http://www.ala.org/ acrl/nili/nili.html.

Brown, Robert D., and Lu Ann Krager. 1985. Ethical issues in graduate education: Faculty and student responsibilities. *Journal of Higher Education* 56:403-18.

Bruce, Christine S. 1996. Information literacy: A phenomenography. Ph.D. diss., University of New England, Aarmidale.

―――. 1997. *The seven faces of information literacy.* Adelaide, Australia: Auslib Press.

Buntrock, Robert E. 1988. Disk-based search demos and tutorials: STN mentor. *Database* 11:87-88.

Burns, Charles A., ed. 1992. *Colleague: An annual collection of articles on academic and administrative issues facing community colleges of the State University of New York.* Albany: State University of New York. ERIC, ED 342454.

Bush, Vannevar. 1945. As we may think. *Atlantic Monthly* 176 (July): 101-8.

Cannon, Anita. 1994. Faculty survey on library research instruction. *Reference Quarterly* 33:524-41.

Carter, Eleanor M. 1986. Adult learner perceptions of library instructional services in public two-year colleges. Ph.D. diss., Columbia University, N.Y.

Cleverdon, Cyril W., and Michael E. Keen. 1966. *Factors determining the performance of indexing systems.* Vol. 1: *Design,* Vol. 2: *Results.* Cranfield, Bedford, England: Aslib Cranfield Research Project.

Cole, Karen S. 1992. Doctoral students in education and selecting resources for the literature review. Ph.D. diss., Kansas State University.

Compton, Mary L. 1989. A study of the information resources and library resources used by doctoral students in science education at the University of Georgia. Master's thesis, University of Georgia, ERIC, ED 313041.

Cool, Colleen, Nicholas J. Belkin, Ophir Frieder, Paul B. Kantor. 1993. Characteristics of text affecting relevance judgments. In *Proceedings of the 14th National Online Meeting, May 4-6, 1993,* edited by Martha E. Williams. Medford, N.J.: Learned Information.

Cooper, Tasha, and Jane Burchfield. 1995. Information literacy for college and university staff. *Research Strategies* 13: 94-106.

Cooper, William S. 1971. A definition of relevance for information retrieval. *Information Storage and Retrieval* 7:19-37.

———. 1973. On selecting a measure of retrieval effectiveness, Part I. *Journal of the American Society for Information Science* 24:87-100.

———. 1978. Indexing documents by gendanken experimentation. *Journal of the American Society for Information Science* 29:107-19.

Courtois, Martin P. 1991. Tutorials for CD-ROM instruction: a review of EBSCO-CD's Core MEDLINE. *CD-ROM Professional* 4:105-9.

Cuadra, Carlos A., and Robert V. Katter. 1967a. Experimental studies of relevance judgments: Final report. Vol I. Project summary. Santa Monica, Calif.: System Development, Corp. NSF, TM-3520/001/00.

———. 1967b. Opening the black box of "relevance." *Journal of Documentation* 23:291-303.

Damko, Ellen E. 1990. Student attitudes toward bibliographic instruction. Master's research paper, Kent State University, ERIC, ED 367373.

Daragan, Patricia, and Gwendolyn Stevens. 1996. Developing lifelong learners: An integrative and developmental approach to information literacy. *Research Strategies* 14:68-81.

Dimitroff, Alexandra, Francis X. Blouin, Carolyn O. Frost, Barbara MacAdam, and Carla J. Stoffle. 1990. Alliance for Information: Michigan librarians and library faculty join forces for the future. *Research Strategies* 8:52-58.

Doyle, Christine S. 1992. Final Report to the National Forum on Information Literacy. Syracuse, N.Y., ERIC, ED 351033.

———. 1992a. Development of a model of information literacy outcome measures within National Education Goals of 1990. Ph.D. diss., Northern Arizona University.

———. 1994. Information Literacy in an information society: A concept for the information age. Syracuse, N.Y., ERIC ED 372763.

Dreifuss, Richard A. 1981. Library instruction and graduate students: More work for George. *Reference Quarterly* 21:121-23.

Dunlap, Connie et al. 1976. Reaching graduate students: Techniques and administration. In *Faculty involvement in library instruction*, edited by Hannelore B. Rader. Ann Arbor, Mich.: Pierian Press.

Eichman, Thomas L. 1979. Subject indexes vs. original documents as research sources: A comparative account of text construction and use for academic libraries, ERIC, ED 210025.

Eisenberg, Michael. 1977. Introduction to information problem-solving for upper high school, college-age, and adult students. In E-mail NewsLin [on-line serial]. Available from E-mail NewsLin@ aol.com.

Eisenberg, Michael, and Linda Schamber. 1988. Relevance: The search for a definition. In *Proceedings of the 51st Annual Meeting of the American Society for Information Science Atlanta, GA, October 1988*, edited by Christine L. Borgman, and Edward Y. H. Pai, 25:164-68. Medford, N. J.: Learned Information.

Eisenberg, Michael B., and Michael K. Brown. 1992. Current themes regarding library and information skills instruction: Research supporting and research lacking. *School Library Media Quarterly* 20:103-10.

Ellis, David. 1984. Theory and explanation in information retrieval research. *Journal of Information Science* 8:25-38.

Epp, Ronald H., and Jo An S. Segal. 1987. The American Council of Learned Societies survey and academic library service: How academic scholars use their libraries. *College and Research Libraries News* 48:63-69.

Fairthorne, Robert A. 1963. Implications of test procedures. In *Information retrieval in action*, edited by Allen Kent. Cleveland, Ohio: Case Western Reserve University Press.

Farid, Mona. 1982. Time allocation in students' bibliographic decisions. Ph.D. diss., University of California, Berkeley.

Farid, Mona, Eileen F. Snyder, Palmquist Ruth, and Dolores Dull. 1984. A study of information seeking behavior of Ph.D. students in selected disciplines. ERIC, ED 252213.

Fisher, Jean W., and Susanne Bjorner. 1994. Enabling online end-user searching: An expanding role for librarians. *Special Libraries* 85:281-92.

Ford, Barbara J. 1994. Information literacy goes international. *College and Research Libraries News* 55:423-25.

Foskett, Douglas J. 1972. A note on the concept of "relevance." *Information Storage and Retrieval* 8:77-78.

Foster, Stephen P. 1993. Information literacy: Some misgivings. *American Libraries* 24:344-46.

Franklin, Godrey, and Ronald C. Toifel. 1994. The effect of bibliographic instruction on library knowledge and skills among education students. *Research Strategies* 12:224-37.

Fridie, Stephanie, comp. 1994. Information seeking behavior and user education in academic libraries: Research, theory, and practice. A selected list of information sources. ERIC, ED 371766.

Froehlich, Thomas J. 1994. Relevance reconsidered—Towards an agenda for the 21st century: Introduction to special topics issue on relevance research. *Journal of the American Society for Information Science* 45:124-34.

Furlong, Katherine, and Franklin D. Roberts. 1998. If you teach it, will they learn? Information literacy and reference services in a college library. *Computers in Libraries* 18:22-25.

Gay, L. R. 1996. *Educational research: Competencies for analysis and application.* 5th ed., Englewood Cliffs, N.J.: Prentice-Hall.

Geffert, Bryn, and Robert Bruce. 1997. Whither BI? Assessing perceptions of research skills over an undergraduate career. *Reference Quarterly* 36:409-17.

Geffert, Bryn, and Beth Christensen. 1998. Things they carry: Attitudes toward, opinions about, and knowledge of libraries and research among incoming college students. *Reference and User Services Quarterly* 37:279-89.

Gilton, Donna L. 1994. A world of difference: Preparing for information literacy instruction for diverse groups. *Multicultural Review* 3:54-62.

Girves, Jean E., and Virginia Wemmerus. 1988. Developing models of graduate student degree progress. *Journal of Higher Education* 59:163-89.

Goodin, M. Elspeth. 1991. The transferability of library research skills from high schools to college. In *Current Research*, edited by Michael B. Eisenberg. *School Library Media Quarterly* 20:33-41.

Gordon, Vivian N., comp. 1994. *Academic advising: An annotated bibliography.* Westport, Conn.: Greenwood Press.

Greer, Arlene, Lee Weston, and Mary Alm. 1991. Assessment of learning outcomes: A measure of progress in library literacy. *College and Research Libraries* 52:549-57.

Halpern, David, and Michael S. Nilan. 1988. A step toward shifting the research emphasis in information science from the system to the user: An empirical investigation of source evaluation behavior in information seeking and use. In *Proceedings of the 51st Annual Meeting of the American Society for Information Science*, edited by Christine L. Borgman, and Edward Y. H. Pai, 25:169-76. Medford, N.J.: Learned Information.

Hardesty, Larry. 1982. The development of a set of scales to measure the attitudes of classroom instructors toward the undergraduate educational role of the academic library. Ph.D. diss., Indiana University.

Harter, Stephen P. 1971. The Cranfield II relevance assessments: A critical evaluation. *Library Quarterly* 41:229-43.

———. 1992. Psychological relevance and information science. *Journal of the American Society for Information Science* 43:602-15.

Hawes, Douglass K. 1994. Information literacy and the business schools. *Journal of Education for Business* 70:54-61.

Haws, Rae, Lorna Peterson, and Diana Shonrock. 1989. Survey of faculty attitudes towards a basic library skills course. *College and Research Libraries News* 50:201-3.

Hayden, K. Alix. Information literacy. [on-line]. Available at http://www.ucalgary.ca/~ahayden/literacy/html.

Hernandez, Nelda. 1985. The 4th composite "R" for graduate students: Research. ERIC, ED 276671.

Herring, Doris B. 1994. The role of the community college reference librarian in promoting and teaching information literacy. Ph.D. diss., Florida State University.

Hersh, William R. 1994. Relevance and retrieval evaluation: Perspectives from medicine. *Journal of the American Society for Information Science* 45:201-6.

Hine, Betsy N., Janet Meek, Ruth H. Miller. 1989. Bibliographic instruction for the adult student in an academic library. *Journal of Continuing Higher Education* 37:20-24.

Hockin, Robert J. 1981. Symbiosis and socialization: A sociological examination of Ph.D. Advising. Ph.D. diss., University of Minnesota.

Howard, Dara L. 1994. Pertinence as reflected in personal constructs. *Journal of the American Society for Information Science* 45:172-85.

Huston, Mary M., ed. 1991. Toward Information Literacy—Innovative Perspectives for the 1990s. *Library Trends* 39:187-366.

Huston, Mary M., and Rita Yribar. 1991. Women's knowing and knowing women: Instructional lessons from collection development. *Research Strategies* 9:77-86.

Ingwersen, Peter 1992. *Information retrieval interaction*. London, England: Taylor Graham.

———. 1996. Cognitive perspectives of information retrieval interaction. *Journal of Documentation* 52:3-50.

James, Stuart. 1986. Educating scientific end-users: An experiment in undergraduate on-line retrieval tutorials. *Library Review* 35:191-95.

Janes, Joseph W. 1994. Other people's judgments: A comparison of users' and others' judgments of document relevance, topicality, and utility. *Journal of the American Society for Information Science* 45:160-71.

Johnson-Cooper, Glendora. 1994. Strengthening the African American community through information literacy. In *The Black Librarian in America: Revisited*, edited by E. J. Josey. Metuchen, N.J.: Scarecrow Press.

Kammerer, Douglas E. 1986. Advisors' perceptions of their advising experiences with their doctoral students during the dissertation. Ph.D. diss., The Ohio State University.

Katz, Elinor. 1995. The dissertation: Academic interruptus. In *Graduates and ABDs in Colleges of Education: Characteristics and implications for the structures of doctoral programs.* Papers presented at a symposium at the annual meeting of the American Educational Research Association, San Francisco, CA, April 18-22, 1995. ERIC, ED 382143.

Katz, Joseph, and Rodney T. Hartnett. 1976. *Scholars in the making.* Cambridge, Mass.: Ballinger Publishing.

Katz, William A. 1997. *Introduction to reference work.* 7th ed. New York: McGraw-Hill.

———. 1992. *Introduction to Reference Work.* 6th ed. New York: McGraw-Hill.

Keefer, Jane. 1993. The hungry rats syndrome: Library anxiety, information literacy, and the academic reference process. In *Library Literacy*, edited by M. Reichel. *Reference Quarterly* 32:333-39.

Kemp, D. A. 1974. Relevance, pertinence and information system development. *Information Storage and Retrieval* 10:37-47.

Kester, Diane D. 1994. Secondary school library and information skills. Are they transferred from high school to college? *Reference Librarian* 44:9-17.

King, Donald W., and Edward C. Bryant. 1971. *The evaluation of information services and products.* Washington, D.C.: Information Resources Press.

Kirk, Joyce, and Ross Todd. 1996. Information literacy—changing roles for information professionals. In *Information Literacy: The Australian Agenda*, edited by Di Booker. University of South Australia, Adelaide.

Kirk, James, and Jay Wysocki. 1991. Factors influencing choice of graduate program and some implications for student advisement. *NACADA Journal* 11:14-20.

Knapp, Patricia, Carol E. Ballingall, and Gilbert E. Donahue. 1964. An experiment in coordination between teaching and library staff for changing student use of university resources. ERIC, ED 002954.

Knowles, Malcolm. 1984. *The adult learner: A neglected species.* 3rd ed. Houston, Tex.: Gulf Publishing Company.

———. 1990. *The adult learner: A neglected species.* 4th ed. Houston, Tex.: Gulf Publishing Company.

Kohl, David F. 1985. *Reference services and library instruction: a handbook for library management.* Santa Barbara, Calif.: ABC-Clio Information Services.

Kuhlthau, Carol C. 1987. Information skills for an information society: A review of the research. An ERIC Information Analysis Product. ERIC, ED 297740.

———. 1988. Developing a model of the library search process: Cognitive and affective aspects. *Reference Quarterly* 28:232-42.

———. 1989. Information search process: A summary of research and implications for school library media programs. *School Library Media Quarterly* 18:19-25.

———. 1991. Inside the search process: Information seeking from the user's perspective. *Journal of the American Society for Information Science* 42:361-71.

———. 1993. *Seeking meaning: A Process Approach to Library and Information Services.* Norwood, N.J.: Ablex.

Lancaster, Frank W., and A. J. Warner. 1993. *Information Retrieval Today.* Arlington, Va.: Information Resources Press.

Leach, Bruce A. 1993. Computer-based CD-ROM tutorials—providing effective on-demand instruction. *CD-ROM Professional* 6:113-14.

Leckie, Gloria J. 1996. Desperately seeking citations: Uncovering faculty assumptions about the undergraduate research process. *Journal of Academic Librarianship* 22:201-8.

Lenz, Kathryn. 1995. Factors affecting the completion of the doctoral dissertation for non-traditional aged women. In *Graduates and ABDs in Colleges of Education: Characteristics and implications for the structures of doctoral programs.* Papers presented at a symposium at the annual meeting of the American Educational Research Association, San Francisco, Calif., April 18-22, 1995. ERIC, ED 382143.

Libutti, Patricia. 1991. Library support for graduate education, research and teaching. ERIC, ED 349007.

Lowe, Susan S. 1995. Collaboration with faculty: Integrating information literacy into the curriculum. In *Off-Campus Library Services Conference, The seventh off-campus Library Services Conference proceedings.* San Diego, Calif.

Lowry, Anita K. 1990. Beyond BI: Information literacy in the electronic age. *Research Strategies* 8:22-27.

Lubans, John. 1974. Library-use instructional needs from the library users'/non users' point of view: A survey report. In *Educating the Library User,* edited by John Lubans. New York: R. R. Bowker Co.

———. 1980. Library literacy: Let George do it. *Reference Quarterly* 20:121-23.

Lussier, Thelma G. 1995. Doctoral students at the University of Manitoba: Factors affecting completion rates and time to degree by gender and by field of study. ERIC, ED 382148.

Lynch, Ann Q., and Arthur W. Chickering. 1984. Comprehensive counseling and support for adult learners: Challenge to higher education. In *New perspectives on counseling adult learners*, edited by H. B. Gelatt, Nancy K. Schlossberg, Edwin L. Herr, Ann Q. Lynch, Arthur W. Chickering, Garry R. Walz, and Libby Benjamin. Ann Arbor, Mich.: ERIC/CAPS.

Mabandla, B. S. 1996. South Africa and new information technology. *Microcomputers for Information Management* 13:169-74.

MacMullin, Susan E., and Robert S. Taylor. 1984. Problem dimensions and information traits. *Information Society* 3:91-111.

Maio, Anne K. 1995. The instruction of undergraduates in print and electronic information resources. Ph.D. diss., University of Connecticut.

Malley, Ian. 1984. *The basics of information skills teaching.* London: Clive Bingley.

Manis, Jean, Susan Frazier-Kouassi, Carol M. Hollenshead, and Dean Burkam. 1993. A survey of the graduate experience: Sources of satisfaction and dissatisfaction among graduate students at the University of Michigan. Ann Arbor: The Center for the Education of Women, The University of Michigan.

Markley, Susan B., and Merrill D. Stein. 1998. QUEST: A collaborative approach to Information Literacy. In *Racing toward tomorrow.* Proceedings of the Ninth Annual Conference of the Association of College and Research Libraries, April 8-11, edited by H. A. Thompson. Chicago: ACRL.

Maron, M. E. 1977. On indexing, retrieval and the meaning of about. *Journal of the Society for Information Science* 28:38-43.

Maughan, Patricia D. 1994. The Teaching Library-Information Literacy Survey. *CU News* [on-line]. Available at http://www.lib.berkeley.edu/TeachingLib/Survey.html.

Maynard, J. Edmund. 1990. A case study of faculty attitudes toward library instruction: The Citadel experience. *Reference Services Review* 18:67-73.

McCarthy, Constance. 1985. The faculty problem. *Journal of Academic Librarianship* 11:142-45.

McClure, Georgetta. 1981. Learning conditions at the Ph.D. level at the Ohio State University. Ph.D. diss., The Ohio State University.

McCrank, Lawrence J. 1991. Information literacy: A bogus bandwagon. *Library Journal* 116:38-42.

McFarland, Robert T., and Julia. H. Caplow. 1995. Faculty perspectives of doctoral persistence within arts and science disciplines. ERIC, ED 391422.

Meadow, Charles T. 1985. "Relevance?" *Journal of the American Society for Information Science* 36:354-55.

———. 1986. Problems of information science research—an opinion paper. *Canadian Journal of Information Science* 11:18-23.

———. 1992. Text information retrieval systems. San Diego, Calif.: Academic Press.

Mech, Terrence F., and Charles I. Brooks. 1995. Library anxiety among college students: An exploratory study. In *Continuity and Transformation: The Promise of Confluence.* ACRL Seventh National Conference, March 29-April 1, 1995, Pittsburgh, Pa. Chicago: Association of College and Research Libraries.

Mellon, Constance A. 1986. Library anxiety: A grounded theory and its development. *College and Research Libraries* 47:160-65.

Metoyer-Duran, Cheryl. 1992. Tribal community college libraries: Perceptions of the college president. *Journal of Academic Librarianship* 17:364-69.

Middle States Association of Colleges and School. 1995. Information literacy: Lifelong learning in the Middle States Region: A summary of two symposia, Philadelphia, Pa., March 27, 1995; and Rochester, N.Y., May 1, 1995. ERIC, ED 386157.

Miller, Margaret M. 1995. ABD status and degree completion: A student's perspective. In *Graduates and ABDs in Colleges of Education: Characteristics and implications for the structures of doctoral programs.* Papers presented at a symposium at the annual meeting of the American Educational Research Association, San Francisco, CA., April 18-22, 1995. ERIC, ED 382143.

Moore, Penny A. 1997. Information literacy: Perspectives and challenges. *New Zealand Libraries* 418:166-73.

Morner, Claudia J. 1993. A test of library research skills for education doctoral students. Ph.D. diss., Boston College.

———. 1995. Measuring the library research skills of education doctoral students. In *Continuity and Transformation: The Promise of Confluence.* ACRL Seventh National Conference: March 29-April 1, 1995, Pittsburgh, PA. Chicago: Association of College and Research Libraries.

Morrison, Heather. 1997. Information literacy skills: An exploratory focus group study of student perceptions. *Research Strategies* 15:4-17.

Morrison, Ray L. 1992. The effects of learning modules on teaching library skills to doctoral students in education. Ph.D. diss., University of Arkansas.

Morton, Herbert C., Anne J. Price, and Robert C. Mitchell. 1989. *The ACLS Survey of Scholars: Final Report.* Washington, D.C.: American Council of Ontario Universities.

Neely, Teresa Y. 2000. Aspects of information literacy: A sociological and psychological study. Ph.D. diss., University of Pittsburgh.

Nickerson, Gord. 1991. Bibliographic instruction for CD-ROM: Developing in-house tutorials. *CD-ROM Professional* 4:45-47

Nilan, Michael S., and P. T. Fletcher. 1987. Information behaviors in the preparation of research proposals: A user study. In *Proceedings of the 50th Annual Meeting of the American Society for Information Science* 24:186-92.

Nilan, Michael S., Robin P. Peek, and Herbert W. Snyder. 1988. A methodology for tapping user evaluation behaviors: An exploration of users' strategy, source and information evaluating. In *Proceedings of the 51st Annual Meeting of the American Society for Information Science*, edited by Christine L. Borgman, and Edward Y. H. Pai, 25:152-59. Medford, N.J.: Learned Information.

Nowakowski, Fran. 1993. Faculty support information literacy. *College and Research Libraries News* 54:124.

Nowakowski, Fran, and Elizabeth Frick. 1995. Are faculty attitudes towards information literacy affected by their use of electronic databases? A survey. In *Continuity and Transformation: The Promise of Confluence.* ACRL Seventh National Conference: March 29-April 1, 1995, Pittsburgh, Pa. Chicago: Association of College and Research Libraries.

Ochs, Mary, B. Coons, Darla Van Ostrand, and S. Barnes. 1991. Assessing the value of an information literacy program. ERIC, ED 340385.

Onwuegbuzie, Anthony J. 1997. Writing a research proposal: The role of library anxiety, statistics anxiety, and composition anxiety. *Library and Information Science Research* 19:5-33.

Orr, Debbie, Margaret Appleton, and Trish Andrews. 1996. Teaching information literacy skills to remote students through an interactive workshop. *Research Strategies* 14:224-33.

Osiobe, Stephen A. 1988. Information seeking behavior. *International Library Review* 20:337-46.

Paisley, W. J. 1968. Information needs and uses. In *Annual Review of Information Science*, edited by Carlos A. Cuadra, 3:1-30.

Park, Betsy. 1986a. Information needs: Implications for the academic library. ERIC, ED 288525.

————. 1986b. Information seeking behavior: An introductory examination. ERIC, ED 288526.

Park, Taemin K. 1992. The nature of relevance in information retrieval: An empirical study. Ph.D. diss., Indiana University.

————. 1993. The nature of relevance in information retrieval: An empirical study. *Library Quarterly* 63:318-51.

————. 1994. Toward a theory of user-based relevance: A call for a new paradigm of inquiry. *Journal of the American Society for Information Science* 45:135-41.

Parrish, Marilyn M. 1989a. Academic community analysis: Discovering research needs of graduate students at Bowling Green University. *College and Research Libraries News* 50:644-46.

————. 1989b. Analysis of graduate student research at Bowling Green State University. ERIC, ED 309771.

Patterson, Charles D., and Donna W. Howell. 1990. Library user education: Assessing the attitudes of those who teach. *Reference Quarterly* 29:513-23.

Perry, William G. 1970. *Forms of intellectual and ethical development in the college years*. Fort Worth, Tex.: Harcourt Brace.

Postman, Neil. 1979. *Teaching as a conserving activity*. New York: Delta.

Rader, Hannelore B. 1985. Library orientation and instruction—1984. *Reference Services Review* 13:61-78.

————. 1986. Library orientation and instruction—1985. *Reference Services Review* 14:59-69.

————. 1987. Library orientation and instruction—1986. *Reference Services Review* 15:65-76.

————. 1988. Library orientation and instruction—1987. *Reference Services Review* 16:57-68.

————. 1989. Library orientation and instruction—1988. *Reference Services Review* 17:73-86.

————. 1990. Library orientation and instruction—1989. *Reference Services Review* 18:35-47.

————. 1991. Library orientation and instruction—1990. *Reference Services Review* 19:71-83.

————. 1991. Information literacy: A revolution in the library. *Reference Quarterly* 31:25-29.

————. 1992. Library orientation and instruction—1991. *Reference Services Review* 20:69-84+.

————. 1993. Library orientation and instruction—1992. *Reference Services Review* 21:79-95.

————. 1994. Library orientation and instruction—1993. *Reference Services Review* 22:81-96.

_____. 1995. Library orientation and instruction—1994. *Reference Services Review*23:83-96.

_____. 1996. Library instruction and information literacy—1995. *Reference Services Review* 24:77-96.

————. 1996. User education and information literacy for the next decade: An international perspective. *Reference Services Review* 24:71-75.

_____. 1997. Library instruction and information literacy—1996. *Reference Services Review* 25:103-18+.

_____. 1998. Library instruction and information literacy—1997. *Reference Services Review* 26:143-60.

_____. 1999. Library instruction and information literacy—1998. *Reference Services Review* 27:376-403.

_____. 2000. Library instruction and information literacy—1999. 2000. *Reference Services Review* 28:378-99.

_____. 2001. Library instruction and information literacy—2000. *Reference Services Review* 29:.

Reed, Jeffrey G. 1974. Information-seeking behavior of college students using a library to do research: A pilot study. ERIC, ED 100306.

Rees, Alan M. 1966. The relevance of relevance to the testing and evaluation of document retrieval systems. In *Aslib Proceedings* 18:316-24.

Rees, Alan M., and Douglas G. Schultz. 1967. A field experimental approach to the study of relevance assessments in relation to document searching. Vol. I. Final Report. Cleveland, Ohio: Case Western University. NSF Contract No. C-423.

Reeves, Wayne W. 1996. Cognition and complexity: The cognitive science of managing complexity. Lanham, Md.: Scarecrow Press.

Regazzi, John J. 1988. Performance measures for information retrieval systems—An experimental approach. *Journal of the American Society for Information Science* 39:235-51.

Rice, James G. 1978. An inventory to test library competencies of doctoral candidates in education. Ph.D. diss., University of Missouri.

Rudd, Ernest. 1985. A new look at postgraduate failure. Guilford, Surrey, England: Society for Research into Higher Education and NFER-NELSON.

Rudd, Joel, and Mary Jo Rudd. 1986b. Coping with information overload: User strategies and implications for librarians. *College and Research Libraries* 47:315-22.

Rudd, Mary Jo, and Joel Rudd. 1986a. The impact of the information explosion on library users: Overload or opportunity? *The Journal of Academic Librarianship* 12:304-6.

Salton, Gerard 1992. The state of retrieval system evaluation. *Information Processing and Management* 28:441-49.

Saracevic, Tefko. 1970. The concept of "Relevance" in information science: A historical review. In *Introduction to Information Science*, edited by Tefko Saracevic. New York: R. R. Bowker.

———. 1975. Relevance: A review of and a framework for the thinking on the notion of information science. *Journal of the American Society for Information Science* 26:321-43.

———. 1996. Relevance reconsidered 1996. In *Proceedings of the 2nd International Conference on the Conceptions of Library and Information Science (CoLIS2) Copenhagen, Denmark, 14-17, Oct. 1996.*

Saracevic, Tefko, Paul B. Kantor, Alice Y. Chamis, and Donna Trivison. 1988. A study of information seeking and retrieving. Part I: Background and Methodology. *Journal of the American Society for Information Science* 39:161-76.

Sayed, Y., and Karin de Jager. 1997. Towards an investigation of information literacy in South African students. *South African Journal of Library and Information Science* 65:5-12.

Schaffner, Ann C., Leslie Stebbins, and Sally Wyman. 1999. Quality undergraduate education in a research university—the role of information literacy. In *Racing toward tomorrow*. Proceedings of the ninth annual conference of the Association of College and Research Libraries, April 8-ll, edited by H. A. Thompson. Chicago: Association of College and Research Libraries.

Schamber, Linda. 1991. Users' criteria for evaluation in multimedia information seeking and use situations. Ph.D. diss., Syracuse University.

———. 1994. Relevance and information behavior. In *Annual Review of Information Science and Technology*, edited by M. E. Williams. 29:3-48. Medford, N.J.: Learned Information.

Schamber, Linda, and Judy Bateman. 1996. User criteria in relevance evaluation: Toward development of a measurement scale. In *Proceedings of the 59th ASIS Annual Meeting*, Vol. 33, Baltimore, MD, Oct. 21-24, 1996, 218-25, edited by Steve Hardin. Medford, N.J.: Information Today.

Schamber, Linda, Michael B. Eisenberg, and Michael S. Nilan. 1990. A reexamination of relevance: Toward a dynamic, situational definition. *Information Processing and Management* 26:755-76.

Schlossberg, Nancy K., Ann Q. Lynch, and Arthur W. Chickering. 1989. Understanding adults' life and learning transitions. In *Improving higher education environments for adults*, edited by Nancy

K. Schlossberg, Ann Q. Lynch, and Arthur W. Chickering. San Francisco: Jossey-Bass.

Schloman, Barbara F., Roy S. Lilly, and Wendy L. Hu. 1989. Targeting liaison activities: Use of a faculty survey in an academic research library. *Reference Quarterly* 28:496-505.

The Secretary's Commission on Achieving Necessary Skills. 1991. What Work Requires of Schools: A SCANS Report for America 2000. Washington, D.C.: U.S. Department of Labor, U.S. Government Printing Office.

September, P. E. 1993. Promoting information literacy in developing countries: The case of South Africa. *African Journal of Library, Archives and Information Science* 3:11-22.

Shapiro, Jeremy J., and Shelley K. Hughes. 1996. Information literacy as a liberal art: Enlightenment proposals for a new curriculum. *Educom Review* 31:31-35. Available [on-line] at http://www. educause.edu/pub/er/review/reviewArticles/31231.

Sheridan, Jean. 1986. Andragogy: A new concept for academic libraries. *Research Strategies* 4:156-67.

Simon, Charlotte. E. 1995. Information retrieval techniques: The differences in cognitive strategies and search behaviors among graduate students in an academic library. Ph.D. diss., Wayne State University. ERIC, ED 390394.

Snavely, Loanne, and Natasha Cooper. 1997. The information literacy debate. *The Journal of Academic Librarianship* 23:9-14.

Snider, F. E. 1965. The relationship of library ability to performance in college. Ph.D. diss., University of Illinois.

South Seattle Community College. 1993. South Seattle Community College Instructional Resources Library User Study. ERIC, ED 381217.

Stoan, Stephen K. 1984. Research and library skills: An analysis and interpretation. *College and Research Libraries* 45:99-109.

———. 1991. Research and information retrieval among academic researchers: Implications for library instruction. *Library Trends* 39:238-58.

Stone, Sue. 1982. Humanities scholars: Information needs and users. *Journal of Documentation* 38:358-65.

Strege, Karen. 1997. Information literacy. *PNLA Quarterly* 61:18-20.

Su, Louise T. 1991. An investigation to find appropriate measures for evaluating interactive information retrieval. Ph.D. diss., Rutgers, The State University of New Jersey.

———. 1993. Is relevance an adequate criterion for retrieval system evaluation: An empirical inquiry into the user's evaluation. In *Proceedings of the 56th Annual Meeting of the American Society for*

Information Science, October 24-28, Columbus, Ohio., 30, edited by Susan Bonzi. Medford, N.J.: Learned Information.

————. 1994. The relevance of recall and precision in user evaluation. *Journal of the American Society for Information Science* 45: 207-17.

Sutton, Stuart A. 1994. The role of attorney mental models of law in case relevance determinations: An exploratory analysis. *Journal of the American Society for Information Science* 45:186-200.

Swanson, Don R. 1971. Some unexplained aspects of the Cranfield tests of indexing performance factors. *Library Quarterly* 41:223-28.

————. 1977. Information retrieval as a trial-and-error process. *Library Quarterly* 47:128-48.

————. 1986. Subjective versus objective relevance in bibliographic retrieval systems. *Library Quarterly* 56:389-98.

————. 1988. Historical note: Information retrieval and the future of an illusion. *Journal of the American Society for Information Science* 39:92-98.

Swenson, David, and Sharon Souter. 1995. Assessing student academic achievement: One institution's experience. ERIC, ED 388337.

Tennant, Roy. 1998. Digital libraries: Learning and retooling. *Library Journal* 123:28-29.

Tessier, Judith A., Wayne Crouch, and Pauline Atherton. 1977. New measures of user satisfaction with computer-based literature searches. *Special Libraries* 68:383-89.

Thaxton, Lynn. 1985. Dissemination and use of information by psychology faculty and graduate students: Implications for bibliographic instruction. *Research Strategies* 3:116-24.

Thomas, Joy, and Pat Ensor. 1984. The university faculty and library instruction. *Reference Quarterly* 23:431-36.

Thomas, Joy. 1994. Faculty attitudes and habits concerning library instruction: How much has changed since 1982? *Research Strategies* 12:209-23.

Thomas, Nancy P. 1993. Information-seeking and the nature of relevance: Ph.D. Student orientation as an exercise in information retrieval. In *Proceedings of the 56th Annual Meeting of the American Society for Information Science*, October 24-28, Columbus, Ohio, 30, edited by Susan Bonzi. Medford, N.J.: Learned Information.

Tiefel, Virginia. 1993. The Gateway to Information: The future of information access . . . today. *Library Hi Tech* 11:57-65, 74.

Toomer, Clarence. 1993. Adult learner perceptions of bibliographic instructional services in five private four-year liberal arts colleges in North Carolina. Ph.D. diss., North Carolina State University.

U.S. Department of Education. National Education Goal. [On-line] Available at http://www.ed.gov/Welcome/natgoals.html. Outcome of the historic Governors' Meeting in Charlottesville, Virginia in 1989—the Governor's of the 50 states adopted the six National Education Goals for the education of all students in the United States. Two other goals were added later.

Vickery, Brian C. 1959a. The structure of information retrieval systems. In *Proceedings of the International Conference on Scientific Information, 1958*, 2:1275-89.

————. 1959b. Subject analysis for information retrieval. In *Proceedings of the International Conference on Scientific Information, 1958*, 2:855-65.

Wang, Peiling. 1994. A cognitive model of document selection of real users of IR systems. Ph.D. diss., University of Maryland, College Park.

Watkins, David R. 1973. The role of instruction in the academic library. *LACUNY Journal* 2:8-10.

Werrell, Emily L., and Theasa L. Wesley. 1990. Promoting information literacy through a faculty workshop. *Research Strategies* 8:172-80.

White, Herbert S. 1992. Bibliographic instruction, information literacy, and information empowerment. *Library Journal* 117:76-79.

Wilson, Patrick. 1973. Situational relevance. *Information Storage and Retrieval* 9:457-71.

————. 1989. Awareness of information and study skills in higher education: The evidence from students embarking on initial teacher training. *Education Libraries Journal* 32:1-14.

Winston, Roger B., and Mark C. Polkosnik. 1984. Advising graduate and professional school students. In *Developmental academic advising: Addressing students' educational, career, and personal needs*, edited by Roger B. Winston. San Francisco: Jossey-Bass.

Wurman, Robert S. 1989. *Information Anxiety*. New York: Doubleday.

York, Charlene C., Laurie Sabol, Bonnie Gratch, and Janet Pursel. 1988. Computerized reference sources: One-stop shopping or part of a search strategy? *Research Strategies* 6:8-17.

Zaporozhetz, Laurene E. 1987. The dissertation literature review: How faculty advisors prepare their doctoral candidates. Ph.D. diss., University of Oregon.

Zurkowski, Paul G. 1974. The information service environment relationships and priorities. Related paper no. 5. ERIC, ED 100391.

Index

About the Author

Teresa Y. Neely, Ph.D., is currently head of reference, Albin O. Kuhn Library & Gallery, University of Maryland, Baltimore County. She was most recently assistant professor and reference librarian at Colorado State University Libraries (CSU), Fort Collins, Colorado, where she held the positions of interim personnel librarian and staff development/training coordinator, and acting coordinator of reference services—instruction, outreach and staff training at CSU.

Dr. Neely holds a bachelor of science degree in accounting from South Carolina State College (now University); and received her M.L.S. and Ph.D. (LIS) from the School of Information Sciences, University of Pittsburgh.

Her research interests include management and leadership, diversity, information literacy and evaluation, instruction, user education, library science education, staff development and training, and personnel; and, recent publications reflecting these interests include "Diversity in Black Librarianship: Is diversity divergent?" in The handbook of Black librarianship, 2nd edition (Scarecrow Press, 2000), edited by E. J. Josey and Marva L. DeLoach; "Diversity in conflict," (*Law Library Journal*, 1998); her doctoral dissertation, *Aspects of information literacy: A sociological and psychological study* (University of Pittsburgh,

2000), upon which this book is based; and "Instruction and outreach at Colorado State University Libraries," (*The Reference Librarian*, 1999), co-authored with colleagues from CSU Libraries. Dr. Neely also led the effort to edit *Culture Keepers III: Making Global Connections—* Proceedings of the Third National Conference of African American Librarians, Winston-Salem, NC, 1997; and is a reviewer for the Children's Bookshelf section of *Black Issues Book Review*.

Dr. Neely is active in local and national library associations including the Maryland Library Association (MLA), American Library Association (ALA); Association of College and Research Libraries (ACRL); and the Black Caucus of the American Library Association (BCALA).

About the Indexer

Michelle Mach is currently the Digital Projects Librarian at Colorado State University. Michelle received her B. A. in English Literature from the University of California at Santa Cruz and her M.S. in Library and Information Science from the University of Illinois at Urbana-Champaign.